ASK
YOUR
GUIDES

Also by Sonia Choquette

Ask Your Guides Oracle Cards*

Diary of a Psychic*

The Psychic Pathway

Your Psychic Pathway to Joy

Your Psychic Pathway to New Beginnings

Soul Lessons and Soul Purpose Oracle Cards*

True Balance

Trust Your Vibes*

Trust Your Vibes Oracle Cards*

Vitamins for the Soul*

The Wise Child

Your Heart's Desire

*Published by Hay House

Please visit Hay House UK: www.hayhouse.co.uk
Hay House USA: www.hayhouse.com®
Hay House Australia: www.hayhouse.com.au
Hay House South Africa: www.hayhouse.co.za
Hay House India: www.hayhouse.co.in

ASK YOUR GUIDES

SONIA CHOQUETTE

HAY HOUSE

Australia • Canada • Hong Kong • India
South Africa • United Kingdom • United States

Published and distributed in the United Kingdom by:

Hay House UK Ltd, 292B Kensal Rd, London W10 5BE. Tel.: (44) 20 8962 1230; Fax: (44) 20 8962 1239. www.hayhouse.co.uk

Published and distributed in the United States of America by:

Hay House, Inc., PO Box 5100, Carlsbad, CA 92018-5100. Tel.: (1) 760 431 7695 or (800) 654 5126; Fax: (1) 760 431 6948 or (800) 650 5115. www.hayhouse.com

Published and distributed in Australia by:

Hay House Australia Ltd, 18/36 Ralph St, Alexandria NSW 2015. Tel.: (61) 2 9669 4299; Fax: (61) 2 9669 4144. www.hayhouse.com.au

Published and distributed in the Republic of South Africa by:

Hay House SA (Pty), Ltd, PO Box 990, Witkoppen 2068. Tel./Fax: (27) 11 467 8904. www.hayhouse.co.za

Published and distributed in India by:

Hay House Publishers India, Muskaan Complex, Plot No.3, B-2, Vasant Kunj, New Delhi – 110 070. Tel.: (91) 11 4176 1620; Fax: (91) 11 4176 1630. www.hayhouse.co.in

Distributed in Canada by:

Raincoast, 9050 Shaughnessy St, Vancouver, BC V6P 6E5. Tel.: (1) 604 323 7100; Fax: (1) 604 323 2600

A catalogue record for this book is available from the British Library.

ISBN 978-1-4019-1615-2

Printed and bound in Great Britain by CPI Bookmarque, Croydon, CR0 4TD.

To my beautiful guides Joachim, the Emissaries of the Third Ray, Rose, Joseph, the Three Bishops, The Pleaidean Sisters, Dot, Charlie, Dr. Tully, and all my other celestial helpers. And to my most beloved earthly guides, including my mom, dad, and sister Cuky; my husband, Patrick; and my dear daughters, Sonia and Sabrina.

Contents

PART I: WELCOME TO THE WORLD OF SPIRIT

PART II: ANGELS: THE FIRST OF YOUR SPIRIT COMPANIONS

PART III: PREPARING TO MEET YOUR SPIRIT GUIDES

PART VI: LIVING A SPIRIT-GUIDED LIFE

Preface

A Typical Day

Last week I found myself feeling restless after being housebound and confined to bed for five days with a wicked flu. Wanting a change of scenery but still extremely low on energy, I decided that the most ambitious outing I could muster was picking up my daughter from her appointment with her tutor.

After I left the house and drove a few blocks, the gray sky suddenly darkened, and the clouds burst with a rare winter thunderstorm. In the midst of heavy traffic, and without warning, my car sputtered, jerked, and to my absolute dismay, died. I managed to negotiate my way out of the traffic by coasting to the curb, and attempted to try the ignition several times to no avail—the engine was completely dead. "Rats!" I screamed, frustrated at my predicament. With a low-grade fever still zapping my energy, this was all I needed to make me feel worse. To top it off, my daughter was expecting me to pick her up and get her back home in time for her next tutoring appointment.

I got out my cell phone and called my husband, Patrick, for help. He said he couldn't come for at least an hour, as he was on the other side of the city caught in the same traffic tie-up that I was in. Hanging up and feeling very sorry for myself—not to mention worried about my daughter waiting in the rain for me—I began to pray. I asked my spirit helpers, my guides, if any of them knew a car mechanic in the spirit realm, and if so, could he or she fix my car right away. I sat very quietly—calming my frustration, surrendering my fears, and opening my heart.

"I know you can help me, and I'd be so grateful if you would. Just let me know what I should do," I intoned.

All of a sudden I had an impulse to rub my hands together as if to generate heat, and then put them on the dashboard. *Give the car your energy,* I heard telepathically. *Do not worry about feeling run-down. Place your hands on the dashboard and let your heart revive the engine.*

Being that I completely trust and accept my guidance without question, I did just that and envisioned energy running from my heart, through my body, and into the car.

It is done, I heard and felt. I put one hand on the steering wheel, took a deep breath, and started the ignition with the other hand. The engine sputtered, then voilà—it turned over! The car came to life and was running once again. Laughing out loud, I thanked my guides profusely. "You're the best!" I screamed. "I knew you'd help."

I sat for a few minutes listening to the engine to make sure it was really ready to roll again, and then, without further ado, I was back on my way.

Five minutes later the rain subsided, and I pulled up in front of the tutor's house. My daughter Sabrina skipped out of the door and jumped into the car. "Sorry I'm late," she said, out of breath. "We went a few minutes longer than usual."

"No problem," I said, smiling. "I just got here myself."

With that, we happily headed home, saved once again by the spirits that assist me whenever I call. Such is a day in my life as a psychic—filled with guides, angels, and helpers on the Other Side who are ever present to make my life easier.

Introduction

What We Can Expect

I grew up in a household filled with spirit guides of every sort. I came upon the awareness of my spirit companionship gradually, being first introduced to my guides when I was very young by my mother, who talked to her guides, as well as mine, all the time. She was the first to let me know that I was never alone in the world and that I had guides who were assigned to watch over, help, protect, and teach me throughout my lifetime.

She conferred regularly with her own guides, and often it was they, not she, who made decisions in our home. She referred to them as "my spirits" because that's what they were—spiritual beings without physical bodies. She consulted her spirits on all manner of things, from where to park the car to what to serve company for dinner, and she had special spirits for all types of assignments. There were shopping spirits to help my mother find the bargains that were a necessity for a family with seven children living on my father's retail-salesman's salary. There were sewing spirits to help her find fabric and make patterns, and healing spirits to help when we kids got the mumps. There were group and picnic spirits to help find the perfect mountain spot for our Sunday outing; sales spirits to help improve my dad's business; and painting spirits, whom she called on when she indulged in one of her favorite pastimes—oil painting. And then there were the Romanian and French spirits of deceased relatives just passing through.

Our spirit guides had a place at the table and were part of every conversation. They were consulted on every matter, large and small, and when we were in doubt, they were often allowed the final word. Because of all the spirits, ours was a crowded home, filled with energy, opinions, and ideas, but mostly filled with love and a deep-seated security that stemmed from knowing we were never alone.

My own guides helped me through childhood illnesses, family squabbles, and school problems; they were with me every step of the way, gracing my days with miracle after miracle beyond my wildest imagination. From my earliest memory, I knew that I had my guides' loving support, I felt protected by their watchful eyes, was assisted by their practical solutions, and was surprised by their bountiful gifts.

Beyond our family doors, talk of the spirit world took place in my Catholic school on the west side of Denver. There we were introduced to angels and saints—one for every day of the year—as well as a personal saint who shared some version of our own name. What's more, we had Mother Mary, Jesus, and the biggest spirit of all, the Holy Spirit.

As kids we went to mass every morning, lit candles to get our spirit guides' attention, and had heartfelt conversations imploring them to intercede for us on all matters, including helping with tests, getting a good seat in the lunchroom, and, of course, winning our volleyball and basketball games.

As far as I was concerned, the spirit guides listened—I *did* do well on tests, have unusual luck in the lunchroom, and win an awful lot of volleyball games. And why shouldn't I? I not only prayed to the spirit helpers and guides for assistance, I absolutely believed that they responded, and I felt their help and their presence. I assumed everyone did—at least until the third grade when my best friend, Susie, complained about being unable to spend the night at my house because her mom said no. When I suggested that she ask her guides to help change her mother's mind, she said she didn't know what I was talking about. When I explained it to her, she said I was weird.

Feeling defensive, I asked her why she went to mass and prayed every morning if there weren't spirit guides to help her. She said she went because the nuns made us go, not because there were spirits.

Frustrated, I insisted that there *were* spirits and told her if she was very calm and half closed her eyes, not shutting them entirely, she could even see them. "They don't always look like people," I said. "Sometimes they look like sparklers dancing in the air. Sometimes they look like a burst of white light, like the flash of a camera. Sometimes you don't see them at all, but you feel them, as though the air is a little thicker in certain places, or cooler and breezy, and sometimes you just feel them in your heart, but they're there."

Susie rolled her eyes, whistled, and called me a weirdo again, so of course I didn't tell her about my favorite guide, Rose, who lived above my closet and looked like Saint Thérèse, or about Joseph the Essene, who walked behind me at school. Nor did I tell her about the guide I'd seen standing in the corner of her bedroom during a sleepover—the one who looked like a weathered, very old Native American woman wrapped in a rough, red-and-white blanket and who smiled at us when we were in bed. Goodness knows, if she thought me weird just for mentioning guides, who knows what she'd say if I told her more! Not wanting to risk my already-tenuous social position at school, I laughed off her comments and suggested that we spend the night at her house instead of mine.

From then on, I began to realize that the rich world of spirit from which I drew such comfort was virtually unknown to most people. It made me sad that the two-way street of communication I enjoyed sharing with my guides was a one-way street for most others. While I wasn't exactly sure how other people had become so disconnected from the spirit world, I was absolutely sure that they weren't better off for it.

As an adult, I've come to believe that our disconnection from the spirit world is a Western soul disease. Industrialization and intellectualism have snatched our center of awareness from our hearts—the place where we meet and commune with spirit—and planted it squarely in our heads, where our egos reign over us with threats of isolation and annihilation. The good news is that whatever the reason for the separation, we can reconnect our inner awareness back to our hearts—if we want to, and if we don't allow our minds to hold us completely hostage. With a little effort and cooperation from us, our spirit guides will gladly show us the way.

What Do You Expect?

To begin, it's important to understand exactly what you can expect when you join with your spirit guides. You see, there are many, many levels of guides, nonphysical entities, and energies in the spirit world, each vibrating at its own unique frequency, much like multiple radio stations simultaneously sending out distinct signals. Not only does each guide have its own frequency, but each person on this planet also has his or her own particular vibration.

Those of us who live in our hearts have a *high* vibration, which is not too distant from the spiritual frequencies of those in the nonphysical plane. This makes connection with spirit guides easier. Those of us who have forgotten that we are spiritual beings and identify only with our minds and bodies have a lower vibration that is farther away from the frequency range of spirit guides, so the connection is much more difficult to establish. This is why some people are more aware of guides than others.

If you think about it, everything in the Universe is spirit, vibrating at different frequencies. We all know, for example, that atomic particles vibrate at particular frequencies, just as light waves do. Ocean waves have frequencies—there's even the rhythm of our heartbeats. Because everything is a sea of vibration in motion, it's only natural that we, as spiritual beings, are able to connect with other spirit frequencies. If we recognize ourselves as spirit, we can more easily recognize the inhabitants of the nonphysical world as well.

The spirit world is as populated as ours—myriad different guides work at various frequencies all the time. Consequently, there are many kinds of guidance with which we can connect: guides who once lived in the physical world; family members who have crossed to the Other Side; guides you've shared past lives with; guides who come as spiritual teachers to oversee your path; healers who can assist in your physical and emotional care; helpers who make day-to-day living easier; nature spirits and elementals that connect you with the earth; animal spirits to guide your path; even joy guides to keep your own spirits high when life becomes too heavy and hard. There are angels, saints, devas, masters, and God. There are even guides—or wannabe guides—who are not on a high level at all, but who are just troublemakers that must be watched. (I'll write more about them later.)

Sadly, I've also come to realize that what is second nature to me—being aware of and working with my guides—is unfamiliar to many, if not most, people around me. It's so unfortunate that I've witnessed others, unconscious of the spirit plane and disconnected from their guides, struggle in fear and desperation, feeling lonely and abandoned as they fight through life with no awareness of the loving spiritual support that's available to them at all times.

Because I've been so blessed by my guides' support and have realized it from childhood, I've made it my life's mission to help others become aware of their own guides. Just as *I've* been helped, I want everyone to know that they can be helped, too. I'm not special in receiving guidance—no one is. We're all Divine children of the Universe, and each of us has a spiritual support system committed to making our life's journey easier and more successful, from the moment we're born to the moment we leave our physical bodies and return to spirit. Not being aware of this fact handicaps us.

The Universe is designed to care for and guide all its creatures: Birds have radar, bats have sonar, and we have guides. When we awaken our sixth sense and learn how to connect with our angelic guides, our lives naturally fall into a pattern of ease and flow during which we grow our souls, fulfill our life's purpose, and make our time on Earth endlessly entertaining.

This book will provide simple guidelines to help you connect with your spirit guides so that you can enjoy all of the abundance, support, and delight you're entitled to.

We're all "trust-fund babies" of the Benevolent Mother and Father God, and it's our birthright to expect a charmed and blessed life. The key to receiving such gifts, however, is to accept that we can't succeed on our own. We must open our hearts and minds to the loving support that's available to all of us. By embarking on this journey, you'll soon be experiencing support, success, and blessings beyond your wildest imagination. So let's begin!

How to Use This Book

The intention of this book is to teach you to directly communicate with your spiritual support system by connecting with the many celestial helpers available to you on your soul's journey. I'm going to teach you who they are, where they come from, how they want to help you, ways to communicate with them easily, and how to better understand how they speak to you.

You'll get to know the world of spirit gradually so that you can raise your sensitivity to the spirit world in a comfortable and natural way. In each chapter, I'll offer descriptions of the guides, explain their differences, share stories about how each type of guide has helped me or others, and then offer daily practices that you can use personally to strengthen your direct connection to your own guides in a grounded and practical fashion.

I'll present the guides one at a time so that you can get a sense of how to experience their energy and influence, and then you'll be taking your turn at trying various intuitive practices that will connect you directly to each type of guide. This approach trains you to think like a six-sensory, spirit-conscious person and allows your spirit guides to assist you in creating a life that's free of stress and fear.

How the Book Is Set Up

This book is grouped into six sections, or themes, starting with the basic tools for becoming sensitive to the world of spirit. Once you master those, you'll learn to prepare your body to tune in to subtle energy, and then you'll gradually be introduced to specific higher, and more subtle, realms of spirit assistance. I'll show you how to connect with your guides, work with them, and then I'll instruct you on how to live a spirit-guided life.

Consider this as a course or training, much like a music-appreciation class. At first you'll learn the notes of the realm of spirit, then the melodies of spirit guidance, and finally the composition and orchestration of six-sensory, Divinely guided, creative living. By allowing yourself to be Divinely guided, you enter the flow of life and begin to experience the magic of this beautiful Universe.

Approach this book at your own pace, and work with your guides one small step at a time. Read each chapter several times if you wish, and then follow with the suggested exercise at the end for a couple of days and see what happens. Each chapter builds upon the last, gently giving you a solid foundation for recognizing spirit guidance and helping you to easily and comfortably trust your guides no matter what you're facing.

Think of this book as a tour of the spirit world with me as your experienced tour guide. Because I've worked with guides my entire life (as well as taught others how to connect with theirs for more than 30 years), I'm deeply familiar and comfortable with the spirit world. Now it's your turn to learn what I know.

When you decide to work with spirit guides, you change the rules that govern your life and allow it to become easier. Through these suggested practices, you'll begin to feel the support that the Universe intends for you. Even though we all have the *potential* to be guided, wanting that guidance isn't enough. Just as watching an exercise video won't give you abs of steel, neither will just *knowing* about your guides or *wanting* to be guided fully open the door. Unless you actively invite your guides to help you on a daily basis, you're going to block the strong inner guidance they offer.

It may feel awkward to be so focused on the Other Side at first, but if you stick with it, you'll soon enjoy the process— after all, guides are fun and have a great sense of humor. Don't be hesitant to ask them for all the assistance you need, since they're there to help you.

Pay attention to all subtle clues that enter your awareness, and don't wait for the spiritual equivalent of Elvis to appear, while dismissing all the rest. Spirit guidance is subtle, so it's up to you to raise your awareness enough to acknowledge and accept their help as it's offered. If you practice connecting with the various guides on a regular basis, you'll soon have the proof that they're on the job, by seeing the way your life takes on a magical quality.

Learning to accept help will be the most difficult part, since we've been conditioned to struggle—we've even glamorized it along the way. However, a spirit-guided life relieves the struggle. So, before you begin, ask yourself, "How good can I stand it?" As a six-sensory who loves living a spirit-guided life, the answer should be, "As good as it gets"—and it won't take long before you'll enjoy the benefits and support you're entitled to. If you approach connecting with your guides with an open and sincere heart, they're going to respond. In fact, it won't be long before those around you begin to ask you for your secret to living such a charmed life!

As spiritual beings, we're intimately loved and supported by our Creator. We're never alone, nor do we ever face more than we can handle without first being given all we need to succeed. We want to rise above earthly struggles and live a life of grace and flow. We want to because we intuitively know, all the way down to our very cells, that we can. The way to do this is simple—stop being resistant, and start listening to the loving support that your guides and the spirit world have to offer. They're delighted to serve and aid you . . . so let them.

PART I

Welcome to the World of Spirit

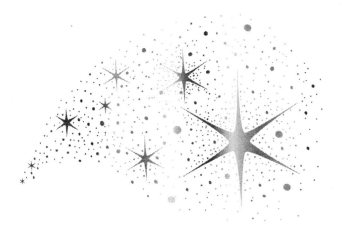

Chapter 1

Recognize Your Spirit First

Before you can begin to recognize the presence of your spirit guides, you must first take note of your *own* beautiful spirit. Learning to see yourself in this way may be a brand-new concept, but it's the truth of who you are—who we all are.

While growing up, my mother often referred to us as spirits, and we did the same to her. She'd often ask, "What does your spirit want?" or "What does your spirit say?" in casual conversation. Knowing that I was one of them made it much easier to connect with spirits who could help me, both on this and other planes. I grew up viewing myself and others in this way, and readily accepted the principle—but the power of that truth was never made more evident than when my eldest daughter, Sonia, was born.

I remember how totally calm and serene, even Buddha-like, she was when she first came into the world. At first she was immobile and slightly blue, but then, with a powerful surge, she took her first breath, and with a tremendous force she suddenly came alive. Her color became bright pink, and she let out a wail to let the world know she'd arrived. Right there, before my eyes, I witnessed her soul entering her body, bringing her to life with that single breath. Ever since, I can't look at another human being, myself included, without thinking that we, too, had a similar moment. Recognizing that it's your spirit that gives you life helps you appreciate the formidable force that is *you*.

Although we all share the same eternal breath of life, it manifests differently in each of us. Your spirit has its own presence—a unique vibration that's totally distinct from your personality (which, to a large degree, is formed as a defensive shield around your spirit). The best way to connect with your own spirit is to start recognizing what makes you come alive.

Begin by exploring what your unique spirit is really like. How would you describe the eternal, fiery life force called *you:* Is it gentle, passionate, commanding, tentative, creative, shy, or playful? Where in your life do you feel the most competent? What activities engage you so fully that you lose yourself? What lifts and inspires your soul?

Next, begin noticing what *feeds* your spirit. That is, what experiences, activities, and energies give you strength and fortify and nourish you at your core, leaving you feeling satisfied, content with life, and comfortable in your own skin? What delights and surprises you; draws you into life, helping you to embrace it head-on; and brings you to peace within yourself?

For example, I'm fed by classical music, beautiful fabrics, and exotic-smelling perfumes. My spirit loves nature, especially the mountains and the scent of pine trees; exotic travel; speaking French; Egyptian bazaars; and rickshaw rides through New Delhi. It also thrives on storytelling, teaching others about their spirits, and above all, dancing. Any one of these activities expands my sense of who I am and leaves me content, fulfilled, and grounded.

My husband's spirit is very different from mine—it loves action, movement, and being on the go. It comes alive when he's on a long bike ride, a summer nature hike, or when he's skiing down a mountain at full speed. His spirit is also sensual, yet it's more organic than mine—the scents and sights of a roadside farm stand, spice markets in the Indian section of our hometown of Chicago, or buckets of fresh fish in our city's market district send it soaring with glee.

Take notice of what fortifies and feeds *your* own unique spirit, paying special attention to how sensitive and aware you are of it. Do you nurture it with the experiences it needs in order to thrive?

I'm reminded of a reading I once did for a woman named Valerie who suffered from severe depression, fatigue, and, in my opinion, extreme spiritual boredom. Consequently, she was unable to get through a single day without collapsing halfway through from exhaustion. Not knowing what mysterious illness caused such a loss of power, she visited every doctor, healer, and psychic in sight for answers, and was tested for everything from hypothyroidism, Lyme disease, and mold and metal poisoning, to the Epstein-Barr virus—with nothing but negative results and no concrete answers.

Feeling desperate, she called me. I immediately identified her problem: She had a severe case of what I call "psychic anorexia," or starvation of the spirit. Her guides showed me that she was an artist and musician at her core, a spirit who loved making beautiful music and creating enchanting gardens. She was a contemplative person whose soul thrived on periods of quiet meditation and prayer. Her spirit was gentle and needed the company of animals, the beauty of flowers, and the calm of a low-key, consistent life in nature.

Valerie had experienced all of this in a small Wisconsin town years earlier, and she had been very healthy and happy until she married her high-school sweetheart, who worked as an airline mechanic and ambitiously applied for new jobs on a regular basis. Since marrying this man, Valerie had moved six times in five years, mostly to large cities where they shared small apartments with strangers because they couldn't afford to rent a place of their own. His spirit loved the adventure and excitement, but hers was shell-shocked and dying.

Because of her loyalty to her husband, my client lost her connection to herself, and her energy gave out completely. Her guides said that she needed to get back to the quiet, natural life and leave all the abrupt and sudden changes to which she had been subject—that's what it would take to revive her spirit and heal her body.

"Do you mean I should divorce him?" she asked after I told her all of this. Not wanting to make that decision, I replied, "All I'm saying is that you should become more aware of what feeds your soul and then do whatever you need to do to get better."

A funny thing about your spirit is that when you become sensitive to it and choose to pay attention, everything in you becomes calm and clear. Valerie heard me, agreed, and listened to her spirit for the first time in years. She moved away from her husband, back to quiet, natural surroundings where she could have animals, walk in nature, relax alone, and practice playing the piano. Her husband didn't divorce her—instead, he worked ten-day stretches in New York, then came back to Wisconsin for four or five days, then left again. Because she loved being alone and he loved adventure, the arrangement worked beautifully. Gradually she recovered her strength as she recovered her spirit, proving that the guides were correct in directing her back to what nurtured her.

When asked, many of my clients admit that they have very few moments that feed and nurture their spirit, and that they just push through life with a sense of duty and responsibility. They feel more like they're *enduring* life rather than *living* it—and forget about enjoying it!

If *you* find yourself feeling this way, know that you've also become hardened and insensitive to your spirit and, consequently, cut off from the spirit world and all its gifts.

In our puritanical culture, where people are encouraged from childhood to put others ahead of themselves and to call any personal interest or care "selfish," it's easy to understand how this type of deadening occurs. Until you reverse this debilitating thinking, your spirit will suffer, and you'll shut out the guidance of the spirit world.

Do You Know How to Feed Your Spirit? Try This . . .

- Listen to uplifting music.
- Sing.
- Take long, luxurious baths filled with scented bath salts.
- Meditate.
- Decorate your home with fresh flowers and potted plants.
- Do nothing.
- Go for walks.

- Fill your bedroom with candles and good pillows.
- Read exotic travel magazines.
- Give your body a good workout.
- Pray.
- Slow down in everything you do.
- Laugh.

Your first assignment is to feed and nurture your spirit. If you're disconnected from, and insensitive to, your spirit, chances are very high that you'll also be disconnected from any input from your guides as well. Begin by paying close attention to your day-to-day life, recognizing the moments when you feel fully engaged and peacefully involved. What are you doing? Focus on activities that leave you with a sense of contentment and satisfaction—better yet, note when you laugh, and feel lighthearted and weightless in your skin. These are the moments when your soul is inspired, and these are the experiences that open you up to the larger world of spirit guides. Be very aware of (and honest about) how you feel when you're sensitive to your spirit, because responding to it and giving it what it needs will leave you feeling satisfied and peaceful.

For some of you, knowing what your spirit needs may be perfectly clear, so go for it and begin to respond. For example, if you love nature, a guilt-free walk or run through a park or a few hours in the garden once a week is all that's necessary to feed and restore your spirit. The key term here is *guilt-free*. If you love shopping and exploring exotic places, then spending a few hours in a new neighborhood browsing through unfamiliar stores will do the trick. You don't have to buy anything—just enjoy the adventure without making excuses or apologizing for taking time for yourself. And don't worry that feeding your spirit will wreak havoc in your life . . . a little goes a long way when it comes to being sensitive and responsive to your spirit.

It's in that initial moment when you respond to your spirit that you'll first encounter your beautiful guides and companions. My mother, for instance, loved to sew, and she spent many quiet, reflective hours in her sewing room, where she often felt a connection to—and even had long, telepathic conversations with—her guides. In fact, the more she fed her spirit and felt peaceful, the easier it was to connect with the subtle energies of her guides.

If you've been so disconnected from your spirit that you don't know where to begin, don't worry. If you're genuinely open to the idea of reconnecting, all it will take is a little exploration for you to remember. The key to mastering these powerful exercises that will feed your soul is realizing that there is no *one* correct way to reconnect you with your spirit—you simply need to become interested, curious, sensitive, and above all, responsive to what nurtures you at your core. Feeding your spirit on a regular basis helps you become more aware of the spirit in all things, which opens the gateway to connecting to—and being supported by—your spirit guides.

Your Turn

Leave a free period of, say, 15 to 20 minutes open every week where you answer to no one but yourself. During this time, allow yourself to pursue a beloved interest, such as playing the piano, spending time in the garden, or simply daydreaming over a cup of tea—guilt free. Gradually add another free period, moving up from once a week to twice a week, then more. You may have to remind yourself to view this as valuable time spent, especially if you're not used to doing things for yourself or taking time to be sensitive to your spirit.

You may also have to teach others—like family members, for example, and especially small children who may not be used to your being unavailable to them when you're around—that this is important time that needs to be respected. I know that this may sound like a tall order, but if you approach this in short 15-minute intervals, everyone will adjust quite easily . . . even you.

You can also try to take a few minutes every morning, perhaps while you're in the shower or preparing for your day, and fill in the following: "If I weren't afraid, I'd . . ."

For example:

"If I weren't afraid, I'd take Sundays off and relax."

"If I weren't afraid, I'd wear better shoes."

"If I weren't afraid, I'd call my mother and tell her I love her more often."

Do this out loud and allow your heart—the seat of your spirit—to speak freely and uncensored. After a few sessions, it will direct you to exactly what nurtures and feeds you.

Chapter 2

Entering the Wide World of Spirit

Once you activate the awareness of your spirit, the next step in connecting with your guides is to become conscious of, and sensitive to, the spiritual energy in the people and living things around you. After all, quantum physics tells us that beyond all appearances, everything in the Universe is composed of pure consciousness vibrating at various frequencies—physical things only *appear* to be solid and separate when, in fact, they're simply energy that is moving so quickly that an *illusion* of solidity is created.

Many years ago when I was apprenticing in the psychic and healing arts, my teacher and mentor Dr. Trenton Tully told me that physical qualities are the least accurate source of information, and they should never be relied upon exclusively to draw conclusions or make decisions. This advice helped me open my eyes to see what is real and true, and aided me in pulling back the veil between the physical and nonphysical worlds.

The spirit world vibrates at an entirely different level from the physical world—it can't be registered by the eye, but is rather felt and experienced by the mind when you start to exercise your awareness and pay close attention. In order to tune in to these vibrations, start by acknowledging the unique energies surrounding you. It may seem strange to do this at first, but with a little imagination and concentration, it will become surprisingly easy. Begin with the people closest to you, such as those you live or work with every day, and attempt to feel and describe their spirit, taking note of any differences you can identify that distinguish one individual from another.

In order to connect with the energy of those around you, simply close your eyes and let your attention slip from your mind into your heart. (Those of you who are natural empaths will immediately know what I'm talking about because chances are you already tune in naturally to the vibrations of life around you, although you may not have fully perceived them as spirit yet.) Next, focus on a specific individual and let yourself feel their unique vibration—including that of their spirit guides. Describe what you feel, preferably out loud, since the more you express vocally, the more amplified your awareness will become.

For example, I would describe my daughter Sonia's spirit as gentle and sensitive. She can be resistant to change, which causes her to be fixed, naturally grounded, and solid. Her soul is strong, committed, and calm, although it can become ferocious if circumstances dictate that it's necessary. My familiarity with her spirit allows me to recognize her unique vibration anywhere I go.

I was once browsing in a department store when I felt my daughter nearby—even though I knew she was spending the weekend with a girlfriend and had no plans to be at the mall. My sense of her was so strong that I turned around to see if she was behind me. Not finding her there, I continued to shop until five minutes later, when I heard her voice. I turned and there she was—her girlfriend's mother had brought them to the mall to see a movie, and they'd decided to walk through the store to kill time until the show started. Just as I'd sensed her presence, her familiarity with my spirit signaled to her that I was nearby as well.

Feeling the spirits of others and of the larger world around us enables us to aspire to new levels of positive experience. My client Harriet, for instance, once told me that it never occurred to her to think of herself as spirit, yet the idea intrigued her as it promised to bring color and excitement to her dreary existence. Although she was initially tentative, she took my advice and began to try to see more than used to meet her eye.

Harriet was 67 years old, had been single for more than 30 years (thanks to a bad marriage), and was working part-time as a secretary for an insurance broker. She felt very limited and cut off from life and wanted to identify the changes that needed to be made to create more excitement and satisfaction in her life. She first observed that her boss's spirit felt dull and heavy, and that his depressed energy infected her. On the other hand, she felt that the spirit of a neighbor who lived in her building was open, light-hearted, and extremely bright—something she hadn't noticed in the three years she'd known him.

Harriet's attraction to her neighbor's positive energy inspired her to make conversation, to which he readily responded. After several lively exchanges—including one where she indicated what a delightful spirit he had—her neighbor invited her to join the bridge club that met in his apartment twice a month. It was there that she met and was hired by a dentist who needed a new receptionist to run his large downtown office. When asked what compelled him to hire her, the dentist confessed that he liked her spirit!

By simply sensing the true energy of others, Harriet had new friends and a new job within two months. By raising her awareness, first of her own spirit, and then of others, she gravitated to a wonderfully supportive situation that brought the positive changes she was looking for.

I've taught classes where I've asked students to describe others' spirits, and their initial reaction was to freeze up. That's normal if the "wide world of spirit" is new to you, so relax and see this as an exciting adventure and not a metaphysical test. The funny thing is that even if your head fails you, with a little nudging, your heart (which, you'll recall, is the seat of your spirit) will speak up and register energy and vibration that you'd normally be in the habit of ignoring.

Claire, a student practicing this exercise, described the spirit of her "very conservative" elder co-worker as surprising and sexy—only to discover that underneath her colleague's tight-buttoned suit lurked a woman who'd been flamenco dancing on weekends for years.

"Who knew?" Claire laughed. "I would never have guessed, judging by her appearance!" In connecting with the spirit of her otherwise unassuming and quiet co-worker, my student was able to enjoy one of the primary benefits of the wide world of spirit: She allowed her spirit to join with the other kindred spirits around her who enrich her life—and even get her to go flamenco dancing from time to time!

Did You Know That . . .

. . . the best part of learning to see the spirit in all things is that it makes your world come alive and makes your heart and imagination kick into full-time creativity? Seeing the world through the eyes of spirit, you also begin to see the hidden connections, opportunities, and support that are available right before your eyes. With such receptivity, it's only another small leap to connect to nonphysical planes and your own spirit guides!

Another method of broadening your perception is to distinguish the distinct energies of your pets. Can you feel and identify the spirit of your dog, cat, or even your fish?

I know, for example, that the spirit of my poodle, Miss T, is very sensitive, humorous, and quite proud. She becomes unhappy when she looks scraggly and is in need of a haircut, and is delighted when she leaves the groomer after a fresh shampoo and trim. On the other hand, my neighbor's dog, Emily, has a far less particular spirit than Miss T—in fact, she could care less about grooming, is quite adventurous, and is ready to run and play at any moment. Her spirit is silly, curious, and far more confident than that of my poodle.

In the 20 years that I've been asking people about their pet's spirit, I've never encountered a person who couldn't describe it quite accurately—much more accurately, in fact, than the spirits of many of the people in their lives. Perhaps it's because pets are so loving and accepting of our souls that we become aware of and sensitive to theirs as well.

Now try to stretch your awareness even further and see if you can sense the spirit in your houseplants and garden flora. Do you notice any difference between the spirit of a healthy plant and that of one that's dying, of an orchid versus a lily, or a potted plant as opposed to one that grows freely? Your mind may reject these attempts as silly, but rest assured that you aren't making things up when you pay attention to the spirit level of any and all things.

With a little attention and practice, all of your senses can be trained to access the spirit world's subtle planes of energy, allowing you to enjoy every aspect of your life in new ways. I remember, for example, taking a music-appreciation course in college and having an incredible breakthrough in my awareness after a few short weeks. I'd always loved listening to music, but the instruments had generally blurred together in a solid mass of sound and rhythm. But as the course directed my attention to the subtleties of what was being played, I began to identify separate instruments and rhythms, thus making my enjoyment of the compositions infinitely deeper and more rewarding.

The same thing happened when I took a French-cooking class. I've always loved French cuisine, especially the delicious sauces it's famous for, but before I took the course, I could never distinguish the nuances of the spices and the savory ingredients that made them so fabulous. Suddenly, I acquired a whole new level of appreciation and awareness of the distinct flavors in the food, transforming my French-food indulgences into a more discerning and satisfying experience. My new awareness no longer made it possible for me to wolf down just anything without paying attention to its energy and vibration.

You can obtain similar results by training yourself to identify the energies all around you and by sensing the vibrations with your heart. With effort and attention, you can *feel* the following: the delicate sweetness of a baby, instead of just seeing her dirty face; the hearty enthusiasm of a young German shepherd, instead of just hearing its growl; and the solid stoicism of an oak tree, instead of just seeing its looming form. At first it may feel as if you're fishing in unfamiliar waters, but eventually tuning in to the spirit of the world around you will become second nature. Like the cooking or music-appreciation courses I took, it will make you feel much more in sync with your surroundings.

Your Turn

Start noticing the spirit of everyone and everything around you, and see if you can articulate how their spirit energy feels.

If you're the type of person who tends to get stuck in your head and disconnected from your feeling center, this may feel a little awkward at first, so start by describing others' spirits in simple terms such as "light," "heavy," "quick," "steady," "bright," or "dull." Let your heart express itself as your imagination guides the experience, and don't censor your impressions. The trick here is to bypass your brain and let your feelings bubble up directly from your heart to your mouth. You may even speak words that you don't consciously register.

Now that you've been introduced to the world of spirit, let's move on to meet your most basic spirit guides: your angels.

PART II

Angels: The First of Your Spirit Companions

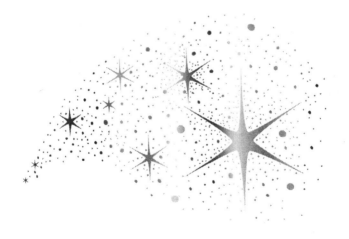

Chapter 3

Guardian Angels— Your Personal Bodyguards

Once you've become aware of the spirit in all things, you'll begin to view the Universe at large as a beautiful, nurturing, positive place where everything and everyone is looked after and loved . . . and that includes you. Just as all beings have spirits that protect them, you also have your own psychic support system, consisting of many different levels of entities and spiritual forces. The very first group of companions sent to help you are angels, in particular, your personal guardian angel.

Guardian angels are very significant to human beings because they're the only spirits who are intimately connected to us from the beginning of our lives to our very last breath.

They watch over, guide, and nurture us—keeping our minds, bodies, and souls safe until we're ready to return to spirit—and then they personally walk us back to heaven.

There are various theories about when our guardian angels first connect with us. Some people believe that it's at conception, others at birth, while still others think that it's when we first laugh. I can't speak for all guardian angels, but I *can* say that in my work as a psychic, they've always shown up to announce the news of a baby, so *I* feel that they first connect with us at conception (and frequently make another appearance nine months later!).

I distinctly remember that when my first daughter was born, I was so overwhelmed by just looking at her that I didn't even know for the first three minutes whether she was a boy or a girl. Then, suddenly, I heard an unfamiliar voice ask, "Well, what is it?" When I looked up, I saw a beautiful face with the most brilliant light around it directly behind my husband, Patrick, and it was smiling at us with such warmth and excitement that it instantly calmed me.

Looking at the baby for the answer, I exclaimed, "It's a girl!" only to look back up to see that the light was gone. Believing that the incredible face had belonged to one of the nurses, my eyes darted around the room to find her. However, at that very second my daughter let out a cry—and exhausted, exhilarated, and overcome with emotion for my new baby—I lost all thought of the nurse. Later that day, after I regained a little composure, I recounted the experience to my doctor and asked who the nurse was and where she'd gone.

"Oh yes, I liked her, too," she replied. "I've never seen her before, though, so she must be new."

The next day, when the doctor checked in just before I was ready to go home, she said, "By the way, I asked around, and no one has any information on that nurse you asked about. We don't even have any record of her being present at the delivery."

With that, a tingle swooped up my spine to the top of my head and worked its way back down, and I swear that right then, my newborn daughter smiled. I knew at that moment that her guardian angel was with us. With a burst of confidence, ready to embark on the new adventure of motherhood, I turned to Patrick and said, "Let's go home."

Did You Know That . . .

. . . angels are a major force in every faith tradition, and are probably one of the few things that all world religions agree on?

. . . Christians have seven major archangels, while the Islamic religion acknowledges four?

. . . in the Jewish faith, Metatron is the greatest angel of all?

. . . angels, in general, are mentioned 300 times in the Bible?

To connect with your angels, you need to give your intellectual resistance a rest, accept their presence, and understand that no one needs to believe that you've had a connection except for you. However, since angels *are* the most universally accepted of our spirit guides, you can usually bring up the subject to just about anyone and be confident that they'll be receptive. In fact, the more people involved in the conversation, the greater the chances are that at least a few will admit to having a personal angel (even at the risk of being dismissed as crazy!).

Zillions of angel sightings have been reported, and chances are extremely high that *you've* had a personal angel encounter yourself, even if you're wary of calling it that. Ask yourself if you've ever experienced a "near-miss" incident or by some strange intuition been spared some sort of trauma, then recall how it unfolded and how it left you feeling. You can rest assured that, no matter how subtle the experience, it was an angel on duty, helping you out.

Shortly after 9/11, I was asked to speak to a group of female attorneys in Washington, D.C., many of whom worked at the Pentagon. The fact that I'm a psychic was already treading heavily on their comfort zone, and not one of them dared to publicly acknowledge a personal six-sensory experience. Although many of these women were obviously enchanted by the topic, it was apparent that admitting any awareness of the invisible (let alone spiritual) world was threatening to their sense of professional safety. However, when I brought up the subject of angels, the mood shifted instantly. Hands all around the room shot up like crazy when I asked if anyone had ever met an angel—woman after woman recounted how she'd been personally spared the fatal results of the terrorist attacks because her guardian angel had saved her.

Gloria, who worked at the precise part of the Pentagon that was hit, said that she stopped to fill her car with gas that morning, and the attendant was so talkative and friendly that she spent almost 20 minutes chatting with him before she left. Those 20 minutes made her late for work and spared her life. When she went back the next day to thank him, he wasn't there . . . and no one knew whom she was talking about.

Kate reported a similar experience at Starbucks. Running late as usual, she dashed in for her daily "fix" and collided head-on with a gorgeous young man who was walking through the door, thus spilling coffee all over him. Apologetic, Kate was horrified as she tried to wipe it up. The man was an incredibly good sport, and three times he said, "Don't worry. . . . I made you do this so that you'd slow down and enjoy life." That mishap made her late to work as well, and she was consequently saved from the horror that had unfolded in the meantime.

Kate returned to Starbucks the next day and asked the guy who helped them clean up if the man she'd run into was a regular customer. When he said that he'd never seen the man before and agreed that he was exceptionally pleasant given the circumstances, she was immediately convinced that he was an angel.

Perhaps these ladies' willingness to speak about their angel experiences so openly was because the shock of 9/11 was still fresh, breaking down their ordinary defenses. Even so, the number of hands that were raised when asked about angels made it evident that having contact is far more common than people realize. I wasn't at all surprised to see such confirmation, since one of the angels' primary jobs is to keep us safe until we accomplish what we're here for, and these women's guardians had literally saved their lives.

Our guardian angels also work with our spirits and our Higher Selves throughout our lives to keep us on our path, especially when we become mired in self-doubt. For instance, when my client Lisa was dumped by her boyfriend of three years for her best friend, she was more miserable than she'd ever been in her life. While waiting in line at the post office before work one day, she struck up a conversation with a nice older man who told her what a beautiful person she was, and what a lovely partner she would make someone one day. Feeling uplifted, Lisa looked around for him outside to say thank you, but he was nowhere in sight. Walking to her car, it occurred to her that he may very well have been an angel placed in line just for her.

If you're really stuck in your head and feeling disconnected from your spirits, simply count your blessings day by day and you'll see what I mean, since most of them were orchestrated by your angels. Train your mind to notice what good fortune has befallen you on a daily basis, and be grateful to your guides for their help. This may come as a surprise to you, but angels are sensitive and have feelings, too, and although they're never hurt because you ignore them, they do get frustrated. They, like all beings in the Universe, respond to positive communication and affirmation, so the more accepting and appreciative you are of their presence, the more surprises and gifts you can expect from them.

This Is My List of Blessings for Today

- I'm grateful that I was able to sleep in late.
- I'm grateful that my computer fixed itself after the e-mail stopped working.
- I'm grateful that both of my parents are alive and in good health.
- I'm grateful for all the wonderful clients and loved ones who helped me raise money for a friend in need.
- I'm grateful that my car repair was entirely under warranty.
- I'm grateful that my dog, Miss T, found her way home after she escaped from the groomer.
- I'm grateful for the neighbor who watered my lawn.

The first thing you'll notice when you start to count your blessings is that your angels are the psychic equivalents of the police, constantly protecting and sheltering you from all manner of harm.

I had a client named Debbie who told me an angel story concerning her three-month-old daughter, Victoria. Visiting Los Angeles with her husband, Debbie ordered a crib and put it in the front room of their two-room hotel suite. That night a severe earthquake rocked the city and everything in the room fell, including plaster, overhead light fixtures, and windows.

Panicked, the parents scrambled out of bed and raced to their baby's crib. Chunks of the ceiling littered their path, and the chandelier that was directly above the crib had fallen and lay shattered on the floor, but the crib was untouched, and the baby slept soundly through the upheaval. The only thing on or near Victoria was a small white feather. Debbie and her husband grabbed their daughter and sobbed with gratitude for her angel's protection.

Another fact about angels is that they're the only spirit helpers with the power to materialize, and they often do so as they work to keep you nurtured and safe. Sometimes they show up to save your life, to protect you from heartbreak and despair, or just to make life's more difficult challenges easier to cope with. Although you only have one guardian angel, it can reveal itself in any number of costumes, at any age, and in all shapes and skin colors. You see, contrary to popular belief, guardian angels don't necessarily appear with silver, flowing robes or flaxen hair—sometimes they look like homeless people or rock stars.

Incidentally, children have a far greater chance of consciously connecting and interacting with their angels than adults do because their hearts are so open and their spirits are so strong. In fact, kids are even taught angel-invoking prayers, but adults believe themselves to be too sophisticated for such intimacies.

Both of my daughters had a string of angel encounters when they were young. When Sabrina was around three and very ill, she reported that her guardian angel brought in many baby angels for a parade to cheer her up. I sat on her bed with her while they danced around her room, and listened to her squeal with delight as she grabbed my arm and asked, "Do you see the baby angels? Do you see them?" Sick with worry for her at the time, I unfortunately didn't, but when I saw her joy, a wave of lightness swept through me. Although I didn't actually witness the angels, I certainly felt them, and the experience left me feeling calm and confident that Sabrina would recover that night, which she did.

Sabrina was 11 years old when, once again, her angel intervened to bring a little joy to an otherwise miserable situation. During Christmas break, my husband and I gave her permission to go on an unsupervised trip to the mall with her friends to have dinner and see a movie. Feeling rather adult and very excited about her new freedom, she loaded up her Christmas purse—with all of the gift cards she'd received as presents and the $20 we gave her—and set out. Despite my warnings to pay attention and keep an eye on her purse, she became so engrossed in the movie that she left it on her seat. The minute she hit the lobby, she remembered and dashed back to retrieve it, but it was gone . . . and to make matters worse, her friends laughed at her instead of empathizing.

When my husband and I arrived minutes after Sabrina phoned us, we found her inconsolable, ashamed about her error, and grieving over the loss of what amounted to her entire Christmas stash. Torn between sympathy for her predicament and irritation at her carelessness, we started to walk our sobbing daughter to the car.

Suddenly, a young girl who was the mirror image of Sabrina darted out of a group of kids and ran over to her. Looking straight at us, she said, "Excuse me," and pulled Sabrina aside, asking, "Are you okay? I know that you lost your wallet in the movie and that you feel bad, but don't worry. Just choose to be okay with it and you'll be fine. You aren't stupid—it was just your lesson." Then she hugged her and ran back to her friends.

It was such a surprise, and the girl was so sweet and kind, that Sabrina instantly overcame her grief. She told us that she wanted to thank her new friend, but the girl had disappeared. Sabrina walked around for a few minutes, then came back shrugging.

"She was an angel," she said matter-of-factly. "She told me that I'll get over it, so I guess I will." From that instant, I've never heard another word from Sabrina about the loss.

Was the girl an angel? Considering how kids usually act, I'd definitely say yes.

Very often, your angels will appear when you most need them, but you won't realize who they were until after the fact, when they leave such reassuring energy with you that you can't believe you didn't identify their presence. My client Grace, for instance, had just lost her mother to cancer and her husband to a divorce when she received news that her best friend had died in a freak accident. Overwhelmed with grief, she took her seat on a flight to attend her friend's funeral. As she was settling in for the trip, a very old, fragile, sweet-looking woman was transported down the aisle in a special aircraft wheelchair to take the seat next to her. They began to talk, and Grace poured her heart out to this stranger, who listened, made her laugh, and reassured her that the best of life was yet to come.

All the while, the older woman clasped a very small prayer book in her hands and reminded Grace that all she needed to do was to keep asking God for help. By the time the two-hour flight had ended, Grace was feeling so much better that it finally occurred to her to ask the woman her name, to which she replied, "Dolores Good."

As Dolores was escorted off the plane in her wheelchair, Grace saw that she'd forgotten her prayer book, so she rushed to the front of the plane to return it. When she asked the flight attendants where Dolores had gone, they couldn't tell her, so she raced through the terminal in an effort to catch her. Yet Grace had no luck—it was as though Dolores had vanished into thin air! Going back to the flight desk, my client asked if they had any information about a Dolores Good. The agent pulled up the passenger register and, looking quite perplexed, said that there was no one on the flight roster with that name; in fact, no one was listed for seat 17D at all. When Grace insisted that Dolores was the passenger who got off the plane in a wheelchair, the agent informed her that the order to get her had come from another terminal, so he couldn't look it up.

Frustrated, Grace looked closely at the prayer book to discover that it was titled *The Lord is Good*. She laughed as she made the connection between Dolores Good and "the Lord is good," realizing immediately that Dolores was an angel.

Did You Know That . . .

. . . guardian angels have never been human?

. . . they can show up from the moment of your conception and stay with you for the duration of your life?

. . . they guide, protect, and nurture you—body, mind, and spirit?

. . . they're with you at the moment of your death?

. . . angels are the only spirit beings that can appear in human form?

I met my own guardian angel many years ago. I'd retreated to Hawaii in the dead of winter to recuperate from a long and exhausting bout of sleep deprivation after the birth of my two-in-a-row babies, a never-ending house renovation, and overwhelming appointments. (This is a story I recounted in my first book, *The Psychic Pathway,* but it bears retelling here.)

For the first several days after I arrived in Oahu, all I did was sleep, but on the third day I roused myself and went down to the beach, where I sat quietly near the water reflecting on my life. Although I had two beautiful daughters and a wonderful husband, I wasn't happy. Our lives were stretched too thin, we were over our heads in debt, and all Patrick and I did was fight. Having very little outside support at the time, both my husband and I were overwhelmed with responsibility. It was painfully clear that all of the joy had drained away from our lives, and we were merely surviving from day to day.

As I sat on the beach, far away from it all, I prayed for a change . . . something to get my life back on track. The following day, I strolled along the beach for an hour or so, then spontaneously turned and wandered toward the city to explore. I entered a metaphysical bookstore with the feeling that I'd been led there. There was a single woman working behind the counter as I began to browse, and I found myself feeling grateful that she seemed preoccupied so that I could wander around without interruption. After a few minutes, a very beautiful African-American man walked from the back room directly toward me. He was about 6'2", dressed all in white, and had a gorgeous smile and a twinkling laugh. The minute he saw me he said, "Hello, I have been waiting for you."

"Me?" I asked, surprised.

"Yes," he answered, as he motioned me over to a bin of spiritual posters. "Look here," he said, pulling out a poster of a female angel collapsed on the beach. "This is you."

"Very perceptive," I laughed. "I *do* feel like that right now."

"Now look here," he continued. "This is what you must do." He pulled out another poster, this time of a male angel embracing the female angel, and flying toward heaven.

I suddenly felt a sad twinge of pain, realizing how far apart Patrick and I had drifted. We were both working so much that we rarely saw each other anymore, and when we did we were hardly in the mood to listen to each other or spend time together. To top it all off, neither of us had any time to ourselves, let alone the opportunity to enjoy our daughters.

"Connect with your partner and remember to dance," the man said, smiling as he swayed to the back room. Before he disappeared behind the curtain, he turned around one last time and said, "I will be back."

I stood there holding the two posters, puzzling over what he'd just said, when the woman behind the counter asked me if I needed help.

"No, thank you," I answered. "The gentleman in the back room has helped me quite a bit already."

She frowned and said, "Gentleman? What gentleman?"

"The one who just walked into the back room," I answered.

Shaking her head at me as though I were nuts, she said, "There's no one else working here." After ducking into the back room to check for herself, she emerged (still shaking her head) and reaffirmed, "There's no one there."

Confused, I looked down at the angel posters. Then I remembered the man's shimmering all-white outfit, and I knew in that instant that *he* was an angel . . . *my* angel. He had stepped in out of nowhere to bring me the message to relax, simplify my life, enjoy Patrick and the girls, and *trust* that everything would be all right—a message I desperately needed to hear just then. Because he said he'd be back, I knew in my heart that my family and I would be helped. I was finally able to smile and then laugh out loud as a wonderful feeling of reassurance swept over me.

"Never mind," I said to the woman as I slowly walked outside, shocked at what had just happened and nearly delirious with relief. I was so grateful that this entity had shown up to brighten my dreary life that day. From that moment on, I've called my angel "Bright."

Do You Know How to Talk to Your Guardian Angel?

Try This . . .

Practice saying this simple child's prayer every night before you go to sleep so that you can begin to feel the presence of your guardian angel by your side immediately:

Angel of God, guardian dear,
To whom God's love commits me here,
Ever this day, be at my side
To light, to guard, to rule and guide.

Now that I've shared what guardian angels can do, let's get back to how you can connect as quickly as possible with yours. Aside from accepting their presence as a leap of faith and acknowledging their support by being gracious and appreciative, there are many other effective ways to communicate with them. For example, angels love music, so you can summon yours by playing or singing uplifting and beautiful melodies in your home, your car, or even your office, for them to enjoy.

Also, like eternal bodyguards and constant companions, your angels are there to listen and act, so talk with them directly—especially out loud—whenever you can. For instance, when you wake up in the morning, thank them for watching over you as you slept; or as you prepare breakfast, ask them to pave your way for easy travel and positive communication in all that you do. Throughout the day, you can ask them to stand at your office door and block all negativity; to screen your phone calls; and to ride in the seat next to you on airplanes, trains, and in your car. If you're facing difficult appointments, ask your guides to meet in advance with the spirits of those you're meeting with to clear the way. Continue to give your angels assignments, and don't forget to thank them for their good work at the end of each day.

One of my favorite means of communication with my angels is to write to them. This is one of the most powerful ways you can bond with all of your guides because your hands connect to your heart, and your heart connects to your spirit, which connects your spirit with other spirit realms. Tell your angels about your fears, concerns, decisions, or anything that leaves you feeling threatened or unhappy, and then, here's the important part—*ask for their help and guidance*. Request that they move your body, heart, and mind in the direction of improvement, and that they interfere if you wander in the wrong direction.

When you finish your letter, you can burn it to transform your message into spirit. By doing so, you agree to let your angels receive your requests as you surrender to their support. This concept of surrendering is important—don't play tug-of-war by asking for help but refusing to relinquish control of your problems.

The word *angel* means "messenger," so these heavenly beings consider it one of their primary missions to support and help you in your communication with the spirit realm. Regard your prayers as commissions to be delivered to the Divine Mother, Father, and Holy Spirit, and pray that your angels take them where they need to go—then trust them because they know what they're doing.

Finally, don't forget to share your successes with your angels, since they're your most intimate champions and rejoice in your achievements while aiding you in future projects and endeavors.

We're not used to feeling good about ourselves because we've been told it's selfish—but it isn't. As spiritual beings, it's healthy and important to be joyful in our successes and accomplishments, and since no one cheers us on more enthusiastically than our angels, we need to be sure to share the gold!

Your Turn

At night, just before you drift off to sleep, breathe quietly and pay attention to the vibrations in the room. Your guardian angel has a strong-but-subtle, powerful-but-light energy that gives you the feeling that you're in good company—so trust that awareness. I promise that you won't encounter the energetic equivalent of The Incredible Hulk at the foot of your bed because angels bring a sense of light, warmth, and calm with them.

When you feel a connection, say hello and ask your angel's name. Trust what you get and don't be surprised if, while expecting something angelic like "Dubrial" or "Oroful," you get "Bruce." Guides are practical and will deliver a name that sticks. If you don't get anything today, try again tomorrow . . . I've never had anyone go more than ten days without success.

Once you've made contact, tell your angel you're looking forward to a long and loving relationship with it, that you're open to its help, and that you're grateful for its presence. Try to search for its vibration wherever you go—much like a unique song or perfume, you'll learn to recognize it immediately and with little effort. Once you do, you'll never again feel alone.

Finally, create a signal to acknowledge the presence of your guardian angel. Mine is a wink and a smile, which is my way of saying, "I'm glad you're here." Allow your own spirit to rest, knowing that your guardian angel is on the job, running interference for you in this wacky world.

Chapter 4

The Archangels

In addition to working with your personal guardian angel, you can also receive tremendous energetic support from the archangels, who are considered God's most important messengers in the celestial hierarchy. You can invoke them for added help at any time, and because these angelic forces are so powerful, calling on them is the equivalent of asking the best football team in the Universe to step in and help you win the game of life.

Throughout the course of my Catholic upbringing, I was taught that there are seven archangels—Michael, Gabriel, Raphael, Uriel, Raguel, Sariel, and Remiel. (You may think it odd that all of their names end in "el," but it's no coincidence, since *el* means "shining being" in Hebrew.) Each archangel has a particular domain, so you can attract very specific and potent energies from any of them, depending on the business you want to undertake. Allow me to briefly introduce each archangel to you:

— **Michael,** archangel number one, is fiery and passionate, and is the patron of protection and love. Calling on him moves you to action when your life lacks vitality, excitement, and love. If you're truly ready to face your fears and try something new and even intimidating—such as switching your career or traveling somewhere alone for the first time—you can call on Michael to protect and guide you as you venture forward.

— **Gabriel** is considered the second archangel in command, and he governs the emotions. He's associated with the element of water, and he calms your doubts and boosts your confidence, which makes him especially helpful to those who are wrestling with anxiety.

— **Raphael** comes next in line and is in charge of healing, overseeing its energy on every level—body, mind, and spirit. His essence is air, so not only does he reenergize you on a physical level, but he's also a good resource for boosting your creativity. I invoke Raphael before I begin any writing project to keep me fresh and focused, and to help me create a work that's inspired and therapeutic for all who read it.

— **Uriel** has a vibration that's grounded and of the earth, and he's a multitasker. He greets you at the gates of heaven, is the messenger that brings warnings, and is also the patron of music.

— Fifth in line is **Raguel**—the police officer on the archangel force—who makes sure that the others behave. When my children were very little and we had to travel long distances on airplanes, I invoked Raguel to help make sure that *my* little angels behaved. It must've worked, because we took many cross-country and European flights, and my daughters somehow intuitively knew (without threats from me) that they had to be good . . . or else. In fact, we were constantly stopped and complimented on their exemplary behavior, which the girls loved to hear.

— Archangel **Sariel** keeps things in order, so I used to call on him when my kids were very young and had friends over to play. Needless to say, the children could get very wild and make a terrible mess, and since I didn't want to be the one to ruin their fun (but I didn't want to clean up after them either), I put Sariel on the job. He obviously made an impression because inevitably, at some point in the afternoon, one of the kids would suggest playing "housekeeper," and before I knew it, all of them would be diligently cleaning up their own mess . . . and then some. (I knew an angel was on the job the day that they insisted on running the vacuum!)

— Finally, there's **Remiel**, the angel of hope. He's a very powerful entity whom I've worked with quite a bit as an intuitive guide in hospices, since his assignment is to greet us at death's door and escort us to heaven. There have been many times when I've held the hands of the dying until I could feel Remiel's presence. When he shows up, the vibrations of fear, stress, and drama that come with facing death give way to absolute peace and calm. This is the moment when our guardian angel guides us into Remiel's loving embrace, and in that instant, everyone present knows and feels that the soul is safe again.

Archangels, in addition to personal guardian angels, encourage the development of your artistic talents and have the power to jump-start your creativity into high expression. They move you to take risks and share the energy of your gifts, whether you enjoy playing music, painting, dancing, acting, cooking, or gardening.

Art is the expression of your soul because it gives it a voice. Consequently, the suppression of the artistic impulse is a deep psychic wound to the spirit that requires powerful forces to be healed. For example, for most of my life I distanced myself from music because my third-grade music teacher made me sit out during the Christmas choir presentation, saying that I didn't have a musical note in my body. I outwardly laughed the incident off, but inside I was wounded beyond belief—and after that horrible experience, no one could ever get another note out of me again. Because I was such a good dancer and loved music passionately, I felt as though I'd undergone a severe psychic amputation.

One day I was given a card with Uriel's picture on it, citing him as the archangel of music. Knowing that recovering my creative spirit in that department was going to require some major psychic "mojo," I asked Uriel to heal me and to slowly revive my singing heart. Ever so cautiously, I opened my mouth (alone, of course), and began to sing.

When you invoke the big guys, you get big results, so I wasn't surprised that, soon after calling on Uriel, I met a musician named Mark who offered to travel and work with me for very little money. I know Uriel sent me Mark, who was so safe and grounded in his music that I felt moved to sing . . . and before I knew it, I was singing at every workshop presentation and book signing we appeared at around the world. Was I on key? Well no, not in the beginning, but eventually—with Uriel's (and Mark's) help—my singing improved and continues to expand my joy to this day.

Similarly, my mother lost 95 percent of her hearing from injuries she sustained in World War II, and she often lamented how she wished that she could still hear and enjoy music. She said she'd pray to the archangels, and shortly after doing so, she had an incredible healing experience: She said that all night long, as she dreamed, she was serenaded by the most exquisite celestial music that she'd ever heard. She couldn't describe how lovely it was, but by the glow on her face, it was obvious that she'd been deeply moved.

What was even more exciting was that it never stopped— Mom listened and danced to the same heavenly music so often that we began to joke that she'd better hurry to bed so she wouldn't miss her concert. She'd laughingly answer, "I wouldn't dream of it."

So, whatever art you're drawn to, invoke the archangels to fill your spirit with the Divine energy to express it fully and freely. Then get ready, because big things will begin to happen.

Did You Know That Archangels . . .

. . . are God's most important messengers?

. . . are the power-booster packs of your spiritual support team?

. . . oversee the development of your artistic talents?

. . . are strong, friendly, and kind, and don't have egos like human beings?

. . . love to be called upon because to serve you is to serve God?

. . . can be invoked through chanting their name slowly between breaths?

I often share information about invoking the archangels with my clients, and many of them find that the results far exceed their wildest expectations. For instance, Anne taught emotionally disturbed students in a public high school, and although she was determined in her mission, she was stressed beyond her limit. I suggested that she invoke Raguel to help her keep the kids (and herself) disciplined.

"How on earth do I do that?" she asked.

"You don't," I said. "There's probably nothing here that will help. But Raguel isn't *on Earth*—he's in heaven—and he packs a potent energy, so try."

Anne called on Raguel all weekend long and "downloaded" her frustrations, simply asking that he help keep things calm so that she could teach instead of referee for a change.

The following Monday she was met by the principal, who told her that their school had been targeted by the city to try some new classroom strategies, since the ones that were in place were failing. The first change they'd decided on was to cut her group of 29 kids into three smaller groups. She couldn't believe her eyes when, five minutes later, 20 of the biggest troublemakers in her class were marched out of her room, leaving her to work with the remaining 9, who were very manageable by comparison.

"Was it Raguel?" she asked me.

"Anne, this is the Chicago public school system we're talking about," I reminded her, as we both laughed. "Wouldn't you say that what happened had to have been orchestrated by someone with supernatural clout?"

How to Invoke the Archangels

I was taught that invoking archangels is best done in a particular way. Of course, prayer always gets their attention, but the preferred method is to summon them by chanting their names in a songlike manner like this:

[breathe] *Mich-ael* [breathe and rest]
[breathe] *Ga-bri-el* [breathe and rest]

[breathe] *Raph-ae-el* [breathe and rest]
[breathe] *U-ri-el* [breathe and rest]
[breathe] *Rag-u-el* [breathe and rest]
[breathe] *Sar-i-el* [breathe and rest]
[breathe] *Rem-i-el* [breathe and rest]

Breathe and chant each archangel's name, and then start over and do it again until you feel them. The longer you chant, the more you'll be able to feel their presence. You don't need to rush—just be patient and they'll come. You'll know they're with you because their vibration commands respect and feels powerful (as though they mean business), but not scary. You'll not only feel their vibration, you'll see their results.

If you have a specific request of *one* of the archangels, you can call to that angel directly by repeating its name between breaths. Regardless of whether you want to invoke an individual entity or the whole group, be sure that you mean business. Remember that God helps those who help themselves, so until you're ready to take the necessary steps to make things happen, even the archangels can't assist you. The decision part is up to you.

Archangels are the power-booster battery pack of your spiritual support team. Keep in mind when working with guardian angels and spirit guides that they don't have the ability to give you the energy you need to make changes—only archangels do. They alone can catapult you forward, but only when you're ready to do so.

This reminds me of my client Heather, who wanted to tap in to her creative-writing ability and talked incessantly about writing a book "one day." As she broached the topic for the 164th time, I asked her why she hadn't started, and when she finally would. She confided that this indeed was her heart's desire, but she couldn't seem to find the time, let alone the energy, to begin—although she'd written her book many times in her mind.

Since I'd been in Heather's "woulda, coulda, shoulda" writing shoes many times, I shared my secret of invoking Raphael to move me to action. Intrigued, she asked me to show her how, so I taught her to "chant him in" and told her to let me know what happened.

Three months later I ran into her, and when I asked about her progress, Heather rolled her eyes in response and said, "You can't imagine! Ever since I took your advice and chanted for Raphael, I haven't missed a day of writing. Something greater than me gets me into my chair every day and won't let me go until I've written for at least an hour. I can't do another thing until I'm done. I'm actually birthing a book."

"Yep, that's Raphael," I said. "Ask, but be sure that you mean it!"

That's the beauty of connecting with the archangels— they make you act and keep you from wasting time. Unlike your guardian angel, who protects you and runs interference, archangels are the quarterbacks of your spiritual guidance team, and they're exciting to play with.

Charlie Goodman, my first metaphysical teacher and the man who first introduced me to the psychic arts, taught me a wonderful ritual to invoke the archangels whenever I leave the house. First, I envision my guardian angel, Bright, holding my hand. Then, chanting the archangels in one at a time, I ask Michael to walk at my right side and Gabriel to walk on my left. Next I invoke Uriel to lead the way and Raphael to get behind me to watch my back and motivate me. Finally, I place Raguel above my head for order and Sariel by my side, and with my "archies" (as I lovingly call them) in place, I venture forth.

This ritual has given me the confidence and energy to face anything. I've even named my VW Beetle the "Archie-Mobile," and I envision the wheels representing Michael, Gabriel, Uriel, and Raphael, with Raguel on the sunroof, Sariel on the brakes, and Bright in the passenger's seat. With such company, I feel that I can travel safely along any road—and so far, I have.

Invoking the archangels revs up our own vibration and expands our aura. Because of this, I call on the archies to go with me onstage whenever I speak to give me a stronger presence. And I always ask them to be in my office when I do readings because they help me keep my energy up when doing such hard and often-draining work. I also place them on the four corners on the roof at night to renew my family's spirits, and I take them with me when I travel, especially when I teach extended workshops. In fact, I ask the archangels to surround me at every moment of my life . . . and they do.

Your Turn

Practice invoking the archangels, and see what happens. Unlike your guardian angel, whose calm presence is like a quiet companion, their energy readies you for action. They give out such a reassuring vibration that all fear and anxiety immediately gives way to bright confidence.

Although strong, archangels are kind and friendly, and they've never been earthbound, so they don't have egos like we do. They love to be called upon, since their desire is to help us in all honorable causes—after all, serving our greater good serves God as well.

One fun way to connect with the archangels is to draw or paint them. I doubt there's a person alive who didn't draw dozens of angels as a child. When I was a kid they were one of my favorite subjects! Even cartoon drawings work, so by all means, use your creativity and remember that we should enjoy our angel renditions.

This exercise helps us make direct contact with the angels because our hands disconnect us from our ego and wire us to our heart—where we have the most direct and intimate contact with our angelic friends and helpers.

Doodle angels whenever you need their support, and their assistance will immediately flow toward you. In fact, try it now and see for yourself how your energy improves.

Chapter 5

The Ministry of Angels

Remember that you're a Divine child of God who is precious and loved, and that the angels are here to serve you according to His plan. You've been blessed with all of the resources that are necessary to live a peaceful, prosperous, and protected life. To that end, your angelic support system not only includes your personal guardian angel and the power-packed archangels, but you also have immediate and direct access to what's known as the ministry of angels for specific assistance and support in virtually every area of your life.

Working with the ministry can be really fun, since as "deliverers of goodness," they take great joy in bearing gifts, bringing surprises, delighting our senses, and easing our way. There are infinite departments in the angel ministry, such as parking, computers, shopping, sewing, traveling, office, healing, and so forth—where there's a need, there are angels to serve. The ministry is available 24/7 and will mobilize into action immediately when we call on them for help. The only stipulation is that our needs are benign and aren't harmful to anyone else . . . beyond that, we're free to enjoy their blessings!

The Ministry at Work

My mother started sewing at a very young age, and has come to love it more than any other creative endeavor. As she says, "It's my time to tune the world out and talk to God." Because of this, she has a particularly close association with the sewing angels, whom she calls on to help her find beautiful fabrics, to inspire her when she gets stuck on a pattern, and to aid her when she has difficulty creating what she envisions.

Twenty-five years ago, Mom offered to make my wedding dress, and she invoked her sewing angels for help. She excitedly called me after they'd led her to the back of a small fabric store she'd never visited before. There, amidst a large stack of neglected remnants, she found a bolt of intricately hand-beaded silk fabric from Italy that was perfect for the bodice of my gown. As if that weren't enough of a surprise, she looked at the price tag to find that the fabric, which normally would have cost anywhere from $200 to $500 per yard, was only $25 per yard! Unable to believe her eyes, she took it to the front of the store and said to the owner, "I'm afraid to ask, but is this the right price for this fabric?"

"No, actually, it isn't," he'd replied. "It's been reduced again. I've been meaning to mark it down to $12.50 a yard for some time, but haven't gotten around to it. As you can see, it's gorgeous fabric, but it's been sitting here forever, and I want to move it. In fact, if you like it, I'll give you the entire bolt for $100."

Mom told me that she'd been speechless for about five seconds, cradling the more than $2,000 worth of fabric in her arms, before she blurted out, "You've got a deal. I'll take it!"

Needless to say, I was overjoyed to hear her story, and even more thrilled when she presented me with the most elegant wedding gown (with matching gloves!) I could have ever imagined. Once again, my mom's angels came through with the perfect surprise to nurture her creativity and add to her joy.

My husband, Patrick, has a close relationship with another very specific group from the ministry: the bargain angels. It could be that he forged this relationship early in life—while growing up in a large family of limited means, where bargains were the only way to afford anything—but regardless of the reason, I know of no other person who has his kind of luck for being in the right place at the right time and for hitting the sale of the century.

His bargain angels love blessing him with wonderful surprises on a regular basis, and have for a long time. For instance, they led him to his first car: an Oldsmobile Delta 88, for which he paid only $300. That, in turn, led him to a job that required him to drive quite frequently, paying him 32 cents a mile in expenses. The car ran beautifully for more than 130,000 miles, so he was able to fully recoup his original investment; and, as a bonus, he also earned enough money to pay for a trip around the world—a dream he'd had since he was a child.

One time Patrick was led to a sample sale (before it was announced to the public) and was able to surprise me with a set of silver flatware worth $1,200 that he got for only $20, along with table linens that retailed for $700, which he paid $30 for.

Another time, the angels led him to a sale at Chicago's Merchandise Mart, where he was given his pick of Christmas decorations that were originally priced at hundreds of dollars, for a dollar each. He found so many glorious treasures that our home turns into an inner child's playground and a magical winter wonderland every holiday season. On the day of the sale, he came home wearing a Santa hat and singing at the top of his lungs with joy over the boxes of fabulous ornaments and dolls that he'd gotten for less than $200.

Those bargain angels haven't slowed down over the years either. Just recently, while he was calling on one of his clients, the angels insisted that my husband pull into an outlet mall near his client's office. He walked into a designer store at the far end where, to his utter disbelief, he found the staff putting up a display of Giorgio Armani sweaters, suits, shirts, and pants at a 90 percent markdown. Amazed at the quality and the price, he asked the store manager if this was a common occurrence. The manager said that it wasn't—the buyers had overestimated the season and now wanted to move the excess items quickly . . . in fact, it was probably the only time they'd ever do this. Thanking his angels profusely, Patrick brought home clothing he'd only dreamed of owning.

As for me, there are myriad examples of my angels coming to my aid, but one of my favorites was right after I lost my job, when the airline I was working for was taken over and the flight attendants went on strike. My travel angels immediately went to work on my behalf, and three years later (and the day after my second daughter was born), the strike was settled.

The first 100 people called back were offered free travel for life for their entire family, in exchange for their job . . . and I was the 100th person. Not intending to return, as I'd established my psychic practice in the interim, this offer was like winning the lottery. Now I could stay at home, be with my family, do what I love, and travel the world. Do you see how incredibly generous the angels can be if you simply allow them to work their miracles for you?

Did You Know That the Ministry of Angels . . .

. . . are your foot soldiers?

. . . are the deliverers of goodness?

. . . attend to all of your needs?

. . . serve you to please the Creator?

. . . have a vibration that is bright, laserlike, and swift?

My mother taught me to work with the ministry by telling me, "Put your angels on it, and expect good things."

Then she'd pause and say, "I expect to hear about those good things when you come home."

To this day I put my angels on whatever assignment I undertake. It's become a matter of habit, and I wouldn't dream of attempting to accomplish anything without them—to do so would be like flying coach after I've been offered a first-class ticket!

It may take some getting used to, but calling for your angels' help will get easier with practice because, when they're involved, everything goes better and faster. Remember that you can live a charmed life if you simply allow it to be that way . . . and just how charmed it can be depends on how much you're willing to call on the ministry.

Your Turn

Connecting with the ministry of angels is as simple as connecting with your guardian angel—just believe and call for help. The best way to succeed is to recognize that, like your connection to all of your spirit supporters, you're building a relationship with the ministry—so the more consistently you work with them, the stronger the bond.

The best practice for calling the ministry is to start every undertaking with a short prayer, such as, "Ministry of angels, oversee all that I do and make it easy, magical, and filled with gifts. Thank you." Feel their presence as they swoop in to help. Better yet, give them the freedom to work on your behalf at all times by asking them to stay on permanent assignment!

Chapter 6

Living with Angelic Influences

Connecting with your angelic guides is very easy, and with just a little effort you'll become aware of their constant presence. Close your eyes right now and see if you can sense your guardian angel standing nearby. . . . Is it at your left, right, across the room, or right behind you? (Most of the time, I sense my angel, Bright, at my right side; however, he moves when I'm doing personal readings so that he's between me and my clients.)

Next, try to call in the archangels and notice how different their vibration is: Can you sense their loving-but-powerful intensity, as though they know that you wouldn't dare challenge them? (Nor would anyone else, for that matter!) Now try to hear the subtle variations between the individual archangels. For example, Michael has an intense, warrior-like energy, while Gabriel's is deeper and calmer.

Another way to distinguish angelic vibrations is to perceive them as subtle variations of the same color. For instance, archangels may feel like intense rays of indigo, your guardian angel could be sky blue, and the ministry might be azure—in other words, all are unique, but they share a common bond.

Trust what you feel, and don't let your intellect interfere by suggesting that you're making it up. Since you may not be comfortable expressing your awareness of the seers' world, it's only natural to hesitate or question whether you're only imagining these differences. The surprising answer is that you are, since spirit connects with you through your imagination. Nevertheless, it's still a real perception—it's just different from the kind that you've been taught to acknowledge.

Sharpen your awareness even further to tune in to the energetic frequencies of the ministry of angels. Again, notice the subtle differences in their vibrations versus a guardian angel or an archangel. Remember that awareness is a sense like any other, such as smell, sight, taste, hearing, or touch. It takes practice to sharpen it, so expect there to be a bit of a learning curve, and try not to get too fixated on doing it "right." Once you get the hang of it, you'll find that it's as easy as identifying different textures, perfumes, or instruments in an orchestra. Keep in mind that the brain is very sophisticated, and is quite capable of taking in, sorting through, and identifying lots and lots of information at once.

Did You Know That . . .

. . . one of the best ways to become skilled in distinguishing among the various angelic vibrations, as the spiritual forces draw near, is to verbally welcome their presence? Start by saying, "Good morning, guardian angel." [pause] "Good morning, archangels." [pause] "Good morning, ministry of angels." Then pause one more time as you consciously connect with each frequency.

Christine was a client I worked with who suffered from a long list of physical and emotional handicaps and was in dire need of help and support.

Married at a young age to an alcoholic and a rageaholic, she lived in a state of constant fear that was magnified by the stress and abuse she'd suffered at the hands of her parents, who struggled with the same addictions that her husband did. To add to her misery, a car accident had left her with severe back pain and great difficulty walking. Not long after that, she was diagnosed with post-traumatic stress disorder as a result of the accident and her disability. Feeling overwhelmed and alone, Christine found her way to me . . . and she actually had to sneak out to come to the appointment, fearing that her husband would find out that she was seeing me, and then he would hurt her.

As soon as I met Christine, it was immediately clear that she was suffering from terribly low self-esteem. She believed that she was "damaged goods" and that she had no choice but to endure her husband's abuse, since he was all that she had. Upon hearing her story, I decided that the first order of the day was to introduce her to her angelic forces so that she could feel protected and free. At first she laughed at me, saying that she'd have to be really desperate to call on angels. I matter-of-factly agreed, but told her that she didn't have to be desperate any longer—she just needed to call on her angels regularly.

I asked her to close her eyes and call upon her angels to help her, to try to feel their loving and powerful vibration, and to let me know when she felt that they were present. When she nodded to indicate that she thought that they were with her, I asked her to describe exactly what she felt.

After a moment's hesitation, she told me that a warm, nurturing feeling was coming over her—as though she were being wrapped in a baby blanket and rocked. I explained that this was her guardian angel, who was protecting her and letting her know that she was safe.

Suddenly, Christine shuddered, saying that she felt a strong chill run up her spine, and she sensed that a huge presence was standing right in front of her. I told her that this was Michael, the archangel of love and protection. With her eyes closed, she smiled and continued to breathe, focusing on the vibrations, and then the furrows on her brow slowly relaxed. "If this force is with me," she finally said, "then you're right— I've got nothing to fear."

"No, you don't," I assured her. "Not when your angels are with you."

After several sessions, Christine became confident enough to try to communicate with the angels on her own. Tired of being afraid, she called in her guardian angel (along with Michael, Raguel, and the ministry of personal support) every day for weeks—and each time she felt stronger. Sure enough, like a symphony orchestra tuning their instruments before a concert, my client felt her support team drop into her life.

One evening, when her drunk husband showed up and started yelling at her, Christine felt a twinge of the familiar weakness in her back and legs—and then it suddenly stopped. The angels came in full force, and in that moment, all of her fears—of him, of dependency, and of being disabled—left her body. She stood up straight (pain free for the first time in years), and feeling very strong, she looked at him, said, "I'm done with you and this craziness," and walked quietly out the door. Afterward, she said that she felt as though the heavens had burst into song.

When Christine walked out on her old life, she walked into a new and empowered one: She got a divorce; entered therapy and Al-Anon; got a job that she loved in a garden center; and remarried a much kinder, loving man with whom she had a healthy son.

"If I hadn't connected with my angels and asked them to remove the things that were harming me, who knows what kind of shape I'd be in?" she said. "Their assistance saved my life and gave me a son—not to mention two solid legs to stand on."

Your Turn

Sharpening your awareness of your angels' presence is the best way to forge a stronger connection with them. Practice by singling out different vibrations when you shower or relax in a bath. (This is much like running scales on a piano.) Slowly call out the vibration of:

- Your spirit
- The spirits of those you're connected to
- Your guardian angel
- The archangels
- The ministry of angels

After calling each one, pause to feel the subtle shifts that its particular vibration evokes, keeping the exercise light so that it doesn't feel like work. Use your heart and imagination, not your critical intellect. More important, notice the peace and calm that washes over you as you tune in, and let yourself enjoy the intricate and beautiful collection of energies surrounding you on a nonphysical level.

For the next several days or weeks, just focus on feeling your angelic forces and getting yourself accustomed to their loving and supportive vibrations. Practice discerning these energies several times each day until you feel as though you've clicked in to them. Once you've connected with your angels and have become familiar with how they help you, we'll move to the next spiritual level of support and direction—your spirit guides.

PART III

Preparing to Meet Your Spirit Guides

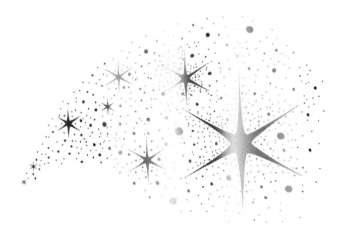

Chapter 7

Frequently Asked Questions about Your Spirit Guides

The number of available guides and spiritual resources that can help you throughout this lifetime is endless. In addition to your angels, there's an infinite number of helpers on the Other Side, known as "spirit guides," who are as varied as the people in your life and serve all kinds of short- and long-term purposes. If you imagine that your angels are your bodyguards and foot soldiers, then your spirit guides are your volunteer corps—ready, willing, and able to serve when you call upon them.

There are several questions that inevitably come up when the subject of spirit guides is discussed, and the answers can be very specific, depending upon the particular guides in question. This chapter will serve as your "crash course" in spirit guides, giving general answers to these questions and laying a foundation for the more detailed explanations that will unfold as you're introduced to the different types of spirit guides in the next section of the book.

So, in the hopes of getting the most basic information regarding the spirit world out there for you to consider, let me present to you the four most commonly asked questions regarding our next level of guides:

1. What's the Difference Between Angels and Spirit Guides?

There are several important differences between angels and spirit guides that include everything from their experience (or lack thereof) in human form to their purpose in our lives, the level of involvement they can have in them, and the way that they communicate with us.

For example, while angels have never had an earthbound experience, most spirit guides have had at least one, so they understand firsthand the particular trials and challenges that we face as humans. Consequently, they're available to us when we need them to encourage and assist us, and to teach us how to grow our soul and master our creativity in human form.

The key words here are *when we need them*. Unlike angels, who are on a Divine assignment from God to serve us around the clock, from the beginning to the end of our lives, and to influence us every day (whether we're aware of them or not), spirit guides, although available, can't serve or direct us without our permission. They can (and do) often succeed in catching our attention and getting us to ask for their help, but they must respect that it's our life, and they can't enter it without an invitation.

Finally, angels have a much higher vibration than guides—since they're so close to God—and they're very easy to connect to. They protect, inspire, energize, and empower us; and while they may influence us through our consciences, they don't necessarily offer direct advice or instruction, which is what our spirit guides do.

2. Who Are Spirit Guides?

Since most spirit guides are beings who've lived at least some part of their existence on Earth, it's not surprising that they've come back to serve us. In fact, some guides may connect with us because they had similar challenges in their earthly lives and want to offer their guidance to ease our way. Still others may show up to help us in certain projects or tasks, because in their past lives they were masters in the discipline we're exploring or working in.

Spirit guides may also be family members who've crossed over and elected to stay connected with us from the spirit plane to offer direction and help. Similarly, entities who may have shared some important relationship or spiritual work with us in past lives may choose to continue working with us in this life, in order to contribute to the continuing enrichment of our soul's experience.

There are also spiritual teachers—who are some of the most important guides—who desire to help us learn and understand our true spiritual nature, all the while assisting us in growing our soul.

And then we have scouts and runners, or guides who've lived past incarnations very close to the earth, such as Native Americans, who help us to become more connected to the natural world.

In addition to all of these wonderful entities, keep in mind that the guide who comes through to assist you may even be your own Higher Self, which is as beautiful and enlightened as any other guide that you may meet.

3. Where Do Spirit Guides Come From?

The answer to this question is also a bit complicated, since spirit guides come from a number of different realms and energy fields. There are also many guides entering the earthly plane from other galaxies and solar systems—some of whom have never had physical bodies—who are connecting with us to help restore the planet to balance and peace.

4. How Many Spirit Guides Do We Have?

My teacher Charlie Goodman taught me that people generally have access to up to 33 guides (excluding their angels) at any given time. However, if the individual succeeds in expanding their consciousness and raising their vibration, that number rises to any amount that they care to connect with.

For example, I first began working with just two guides when I was a very young child: one whom I called Dot, because I experienced her as a bright blue dot of light in my mind's eye (I believe she is my Higher Self); and another named Rose, who looks very much like Saint Thérèse, and whom I feel I've shared past lives with.

In addition to these two guides (who have continued to work very closely with me throughout my entire life), I connected with another guide named Joseph—with whom I shared a past life as an Essene. He's also been around since my childhood, and although he comes and goes, he's always there to help me when I need him in matters relating to physical health.

As I got older and my soul continued to grow, I became acquainted with several of my spiritual teachers. I first met three French bishops who were associated with the Rosicrucians in the Middle Ages, and who served as my teachers in other past lives as well. They will always be with me, as will the two additional teachers I've met, who are from another galaxy and call themselves "The Pleaidean Sisters." I feel that I've had no past-life connection with them, but that they were simply attracted to me by a desire to help me better serve people in understanding their life's purpose.

Recently I've been making a connection with a new set of guides who call themselves the "Emissaries of the Third Ray." This team of guides doesn't work with individuals and generally shows up to speak *through* me to larger groups.

As you can see, not only can the number of guides in your life change, but the guides themselves—and the amount of time they remain in your life—can change, evolve, and shift as you grow your soul. Over the years I've had many guides—mainly helpers and healers—who've appeared, and then left to allow new entities to take their place. This happens all the time . . . it's like a revolving door!

The same is true for my husband, Patrick, who has several loyal and beautiful guides who help him in many different aspects of his life. For example, there's Seamus, the king—one of his spirit teachers who inspires him to leadership; Jean Quille, a helper guide (with whom he's shared many past lives), who works hard to help Patrick retain his sense of adventure and fun; and Larry, his companion guide, who helps him listen and communicate better.

In addition to this trio, Patrick has also connected with an artist named Vincent who showed up several years ago to help him in the pursuit of painting (his deepest love); and finally, there's Mary, who is a teacher who aids him in softening his heart, opening his mind, and understanding all things feminine . . . especially the women in his family!

My sister Cuky, on the other hand, works with many guides who were family members she was very close to as a child growing up in Denver—especially Grandma and Grandpa Choquette and our great-aunt Emma Bernard—all of whom keep her spirit light, loving, and laughing.

As a healer herself, Cuky has also attracted a number of beautiful healing guides—including several ancient Hawaiian and Polynesian healers and warriors with whom she's shared past lives. These entities appear in her "healing room," and she channels them through her body as she works to clear past psychic debris and free her clients' spirits. In fact, when Cuky worked on me (with the help of her guides), my spirit was taken out of body and deeply nurtured and cleared, while my physical body was emptied of all energetic disturbances.

Did You Know That . . .

. . . guides can be helpers, healers, teachers, runners, past-life connections, family, high-terrestrial beings from other galaxies, and even animals?

. . . you have the right to ask only for the highest guides, and when you do, you're under no obligation to listen to any guidance that doesn't feel right or good to you?

. . . the more open you are to your guides and their help, the greater your life will be?

. . . the only function of guides is to offer their help to you?

Keep in mind that some spirit guides are better than others, so it's important to make certain that we're working with the best ones possible. Whether in a body or not, we're all on a journey toward higher consciousness, and we therefore need to remember that just because someone has crossed over into spirit and wants to serve as a guide doesn't necessarily mean that he or she is instantly enlightened.

This reminds me of my client Amy's mother, Maria, who crossed over into spirit and was serving her as a guide.

Although Amy was thrilled beyond belief to be once again connected to her mother, she soon realized that, as a spirit, Maria was nearly as cautious and fearful as she'd been when she was alive. Every time Amy wanted to take a trip or do something adventurous or indulgent, she asked her mother for guidance and could instantly feel her replying, "Be careful!" or "My, that's expensive!" instead of, "Go for it. Enjoy!"

"I fought with her fears throughout my entire life," Amy told me, exasperated. "Now I feel that she'll bug me into infinity!"

Laughing, but sympathetic, I replied, "Why don't you simply stop asking your mother's opinion on certain things? Body or spirit, she's still the mother that you know and love— and if you're going to ask her opinion, don't be surprised when you get it!"

It was better for Amy to consult Maria on topics where she *wanted* her input—such as simply reassuring her of her love and continued presence in her life and in her heart—and to leave her out of any decisions that involved venturing out and indulging her whims, since that was never her mother's best territory.

When connecting with your guides, it's very important that you're conscious of your intentions. One of the reasons why people have trouble connecting with or feeling their guides is that they're too willing to turn over their lives entirely. High spiritual guides—those whose souls are elevated and are genuinely interested in supporting your growth—will only offer suggestions, and they'll *never* tell you what to do. You can tell if a guide is from an elevated vibration (and is worth listening to) if they refuse to connect with you and interfere when they know that you want them to do exactly that. High spiritual guides understand that they're not there to run your life in any way (nor should you let them!), and that you're here on the earthly plane attending "spiritual school" to learn to claim your Divine creative power. Your guides serve only as tutors . . . they won't do your homework for you!

Your Turn

Getting to know your guides and learning to work with them is exciting and will make your life magical and stress free. They want to help you whenever they can and are simply waiting for you to invite them to get involved.

The best way to get started in connecting with your spirit guides is to spend some time thinking about the areas of your life where they can best be of service. Take an inventory of your life and figure out which areas are working and which aren't. Make a mental or written list of what you'd like to experience that you aren't. Where are you most interested in gaining spiritual guidance? What endeavors or disciplines would you most like assistance in exploring? Once you've decided where you'd like spiritual support, we'll discuss the steps that are necessary to connect with the guides who can help you accomplish your goals.

Chapter 8

Getting Ready to Meet Your Spirit Guides

Now that you know you have access to a variety of beautiful spirits who will work with you to grow your soul and assist you in your day-to-day challenges, it's time to start preparing to connect with them. This chapter will give you a step-by-step guide for doing so.

Step #1: Ask Yourself How Open You Are to Guidance

This first step may seem like an obvious one. In fact, whenever I ask this question, most of my clients and students share that opinion. They say that of course they're totally open—why else would they be talking to me? While you may feel that this is true for you as well, I've learned through my experiences as an intuitive guide and teacher that it may not be quite that simple.

More often than not, I've made suggestions to clients that would clearly ease their way, only to have them ignore or reject my advice. For example, I've seen many people take copious notes during a reading only to leave the notebook behind . . . and never come back for it. I've even had clients talk through an entire session, hardly leaving me time to offer direction, preferring just to hear themselves speak. Now there's nothing wrong with that—but it's something very different from seeking guidance.

I've even been guilty of ignoring spiritual guidance myself—such as the time when I asked my guides about a very talented new friend whom I really enjoyed, so much so that I was thinking of working with her. They cautioned me, saying that she wasn't the kind of person to share a platform; rather, she was someone who would want to have it all to herself. Since this was an opinion that I certainly didn't share, I ignored my guides' advice . . . I also ignored my sister, my husband, other friends, and even my kids—all of whom said that working with her would end up being a problem. However, I was stubborn and didn't want to listen, and then I was actually surprised when the situation turned out exactly the way they'd all said it would! I enjoyed this woman so much that I was blinded to her ambition, which in the long run took precedence over our friendship.

So as you can see, it can be extremely hard to accept guidance and support (even for me!) once we've made up our mind to do things in a certain way. In fact, years ago, when clients came to see my mother for guidance, she'd first ask, "Do you really want guidance, or do you just want me to agree with you?" and *then* she'd proceed with the reading.

This is a very good question to ask if you want to successfully connect with *your* spirit guides. It's also a good time to remind yourself that it's perfectly all right to live your entire life without ever asking for assistance or support—your guides will never interfere with you. Just be clear and honest with yourself about how open and receptive you are to help, and know that if and when you *do* want guidance, it's available for the asking.

Another important thing my mother taught me was that I should never ask my guides for input unless I was willing to listen to the answer . . . because if I ignored their guidance often enough, they'd go silent. Essentially, what this means is that you have access to guides, and they'll help—but *only* if you let them!

Step #2: Learn to Quiet Your Mind and Listen Within

Spirit guidance is so subtle that it's very easy for your mind to pounce on it and throw it away as nonsense. Your intellect may also try to tell you that it's only your imagination, and that's fine. Remember that, as we discussed earlier, all spirit guidance comes to your soul and awareness through your imagination, and that's why this step is so crucial.

There are many simple skills that you can master that will help you receive spirit guidance, including deep listening and relaxed breathing. To practice deep listening, simply close your eyes and listen to a favorite piece of calming, classical music without interruption. Choose something that speaks to your heart, and while listening, try to identify the particular instruments. As you lose yourself in the music, don't be surprised if subtle pieces of guidance and information leap to mind. When this happens, graciously view it as an introduction to spirit guidance.

Relaxed breathing can also make you receptive to your deeper awareness, allowing you to open the proper channels to communicate with the spirit realm. You can very easily combine deep listening and relaxed breathing the next time you're in conversation by making eye contact with the person speaking, and if possible, sharing a breath with them (this means that you breathe in and exhale at the same time that they do). This is easy to do if you simply take notice of the other person's pattern of breathing and adopt it—doing so establishes a common vibration and opens both your heart and theirs automatically. This then connects you soul to soul and opens the path to a deeper connection.

Next, relax and breathe deeply at your own pace while you listen to what the other person is saying. Be sure to let them finish speaking before you respond. After relaxed breathing, you may be surprised at what comes out of your mouth when you finally do speak!

Do You Know How to Change the Channel?

Try This . . .

One of my favorite tools is "changing the channel." To do so, simply say: "My brain says [fill in the blank] on the subject." Then pause, and follow with: "My heart and inner guide say [fill in the blank] on the subject." This exercise will help you change the channel of your awareness from your mind chatter to the higher frequencies of spirit.

You can also welcome spirit by learning to meditate. This suggestion always elicits a collective groan from my classes; however, it's a necessary step in learning to quiet your mind and discipline yourself to move your attention to the subtle vibrations of spirit.

To meditate, you don't have to twist yourself into the lotus position and say "Om" . . . you don't even have to sit! I've enjoyed many glorious walking, cooking, cleaning, gardening, and even laundry-folding meditations. The key to my personal success in this practice is that I stop thinking about the future and the past and focus on my breathing as I enjoy the world around me—giving my full and undivided attention only to what I'm doing in the moment. (Thich Nhat Hanh, the celebrated Buddhist monk, calls this "mindful meditation.") Consider this time to be the period in the day when you're open to support and guidance, and tell your guides that this is a good time to check in because your attention will be relaxed and you'll be free to listen.

A further preparatory step is to pray—often and always. You can pray in any way that you like, since it's simply a conversation with God, the Universe, and all of God's helpers. The more you pray, the higher and higher your own frequency becomes, making the connection to your guides much easier to establish.

When praying, you should not only bare your heart and soul to your Creator, but remember to thank It for all of the blessings in your life as well. Prayers of gratitude, in particular, raise your frequency by opening your heart and focusing your awareness on all of the love and support that are already present in your life.

Did You Know That . . .

. . . The more you appreciate how much you're presently blessed and supported, the easier it will be to continue to connect with your guides? One of my favorite prayers is:

"Creator of the Universe
and all forms and expressions that
support the goodness of life, thank You for
[fill in the blank] that You have
blessed me with today."

Once you've practiced the different methods for opening yourself up to the higher frequencies of spirit, the next step for preparing to connect with your guides is to review the areas where you've decided that you want guidance, acknowledge them, and then (this is very important) stop talking about them. Exercise discipline in keeping your conversations upbeat and positive, since it's very hard to tune in to your guides if you're mesmerized by drama and upset. You know the problem—now practice being quiet enough to hear the solution.

Step #3: Exercise!

Surprising as it may seem, moving your body can also help you become more spiritually receptive. After all, we humans are designed to move, and the more we do, the more the nature spirit of the earth can assist in raising our vibration. Look at it this way: The more we exercise, the more water we drink, thus giving the water spirit more opportunities to cleanse our emotions. At the same time, the air and fire spirits raise our consciousness, creating an optimal state for receiving communication from our guides. Many of my clients have reported that they feel at one with the Universe and get very clear guidance for their lives during or after exercise.

There's another reason why movement is quite helpful—and may even be essential—to spiritual connection: The mind wants to become fixed so that it shuts things out, while spirit is fluid and allows things to flow. The more we move our bodies, the more we flow with spirit; and the more we flow, the more flexible we become, and the more easily our guides can direct our path.

Flexibility is an important ingredient for change, so we must make sure that we listen to the guidance that's given to us with a willingness to dismiss the structure that often accompanies expectation. I can't tell you the number of times my guides have given me a slight nudge here or there, causing me to make a move that changed my life.

For instance, when I was in college, I applied to a study-abroad program in France, only to be denied because my application was submitted past the deadline. As I lay grieving over the rejection on the lawn at the University of Denver, my guides nudged me and suggested loud and clear that I go to the dean. If I hadn't been so used to responding to my guidance by being physically flexible and willing to move, my mind may very well have shut that suggestion out. Instead, because of that nudge, I got up and walked into the dean's office. With grace on my side, I had an unscheduled chance to plead my case, and I not only got accepted to the program, but I also received a full scholarship to go as well. Had I not made the choice to listen to my guides and move right then, I'm sure I never would have gone.

Step #4: Stop Playing the Victim

Perhaps the greatest way to slam the door shut, both on your guides and your own spirit, is to say, "I have no choice." Choice is the one thing you *do* have in life that no one can take away. . . especially a choice about how you see yourself.

You can tell yourself that you're a five-sensory victim of circumstances with no power in your life—or you can invite the sixth-sense spirit into your life and take charge of your circumstances through its guidance. If I were you, I'd choose the latter. Recognize and accept that you're spirit and an important part of this beautiful world—you were created by God, are protected by angels, are overseen by archangels, are assisted by the ministry, and are keenly supported by your guides—all because you're precious, holy, royal, and loved. Given your place in the Universe, it makes sense that you're guided. After all, any being as valuable and precious as *you* are would naturally be given all of the resources needed to thrive!

Step #5: Become One Who Forgives and Doesn't Judge

The final (and sometimes most important) way to prepare to receive spirit is to stop judging yourself or others, and to *forgive, forgive, forgive.* Nothing scrambles psychic circuits and disconnects you from high frequencies faster and more completely than being judgmental or holding a grudge. These negative energies not only disconnect you from guidance, they also disconnect you from your spirit, from others, and from the natural world.

I know that this is a tall order, but if you think it through, you'll see that forgiving and not judging are far less work than condemning. We humans are all manifestations of one Divine spirit vibrating at different levels of consciousness and frequencies at one time. Like cells in a body, we're all on this planet together, and when one cell attacks another in the body, we call that cancer. Similarly, when we attack one another (or ourselves) through condemnation and judgment, it's no less cancerous and toxic to our entire being—body, mind, and soul.

The benefit of not judging is that it allows your awareness to be channeled into seeing important things—such as your own spirit, the nature spirits, your angels, and your guides. The easiest way to release yourself from the habit of judging and bearing grudges is to simply state your intention to do so every day. Affirm: *I forgive myself for judging and resenting. I release myself from all of my judgments and resentments, as well as from all negative perceptions. With my breath, I share my spirit with all and return to peace and balance. So be it.*

Your Turn

My teacher Charlie once said, "The best way to connect with your guides is through a keen sense of the obvious." Start to become more aware of where you seek guidance in your everyday life. Get into the habit of beginning each task with a quick prayer for help and support. For example, when taking a shower in the morning, ask for guidance throughout the day ahead. Then, while driving to work, ask for guidance on the best, most stress-free route to take; or if you're taking public transportation, ask for guidance on getting the best seat on the train or bus, the most pleasant seatmates, and perfect timing on your arrival.

Check in with your guides during the day. For instance, when working on a project, ask for guidance on doing it easily, quickly, and creatively. It can also help to consult your guides on what to say (and how to say it) when you're having conversations with difficult people or individuals who intimidate you. You can even ask for suggestions on where to go to lunch and what to order.

On a physical level, it's very important that you remember to bend, stretch, and move to keep yourself flexible. Every morning, take a deep breath and stretch before even getting out of bed; then stand, reach for the sky, and slowly bend over and try to touch your toes. (Easy does it—don't wrench your back!) While brushing your teeth, gently twist your torso from side to side and move your waist, finishing off the routine with a few hip circles in both directions to keep them nice and loose. Not only will this improve your circulation, but it will also make you more guidable.

You can also try parking a few blocks from work and walking the rest of the way to the office—or, if you're taking public transportation, get off the bus or train a few blocks earlier and do the same, leaving enough time to walk slowly and enjoy the exercise and the sights.

Throughout the day, don't forget to take the time to listen deeply and meditate, and whenever possible, share a breath with the person you're speaking with.

Finally, before going to bed, review the day, and wherever appropriate, forgive, forget, release, and open up to high frequencies. If you must, write down any upsets from the day that still cling to you, and ask for guidance while you sleep to clear away these frustrations and obstacles. Go to sleep with the clear intention of releasing the day completely and sleeping in peace. You'll enjoy the benefits right away, and soon you will have created a clear pathway for connecting with all of your guides.

Chapter 9

Making Initial Contact with Your Guides

Once you're open to sharing your concerns, challenges, and successes with your guides, they, in turn, will make subtle-yet-direct contact with you, approaching you very gently at first. In fact, until you become more familiar with their unique vibrations, you may wonder if you're imagining the connection and, consequently, decide to dismiss it.

One of the greatest obstacles to connecting with your guides is having unrealistic expectations of what receiving guidance should be like. Most people are surprised by how understated spirit guides can be. Conditioned by Hollywood and bad horror novels, they expect strange beings in space suits to beam down to them in the night when, in reality, most spirit guidance is as subtle as the brush of a butterfly's wing on your cheek. So, if you're waiting for a booming voice or an apparition of Merlin to appear at the foot of your bed, you'll most likely be disappointed.

Contact with spirit guides occurs on a deep, intimate level—not as some external entity coming at you. The art and skill of accurately perceiving your guides comes from the ability to comfortably tune in and listen to these subtleties and accept them as important communications.

For example, when I connected with my first guide, I experienced her as a bright blue dot that hovered above me when I had my eyes closed, but the minute I opened them, she disappeared. As I learned more about guides, I found out that this level of gentle communication is very common. Most spirit guides connect with us in such a fashion that, at least in the early stages of contact, it feels as though you're hearing your own inner voice—however, the difference lies in what's *between* your voice and that of your guide.

I spoke to a woman named Susan at one of my intuitive workshops who was having this experience, finding herself feeling stuck and unable to connect with her guide. "All I hear is my own voice," she complained.

"Are you sure?" I asked. "What did your own voice say?"

"I asked my guide to give me some insight into my difficult marriage, and to offer me guidance to lessen our struggle," she replied.

"And what did your own voice say?" I pursued.

"It said to stop focusing on my husband and to consider going back to school."

I sat quietly with her for a moment, and then asked, "Is this something that you generally say to yourself, or is it something that you've thought about before?"

"I've never thought about school as a response to my marriage troubles," she said. "I've thought about couples counseling, therapy, even separation, but never school."

"So how does that suggestion feel to you? Would you like to go back to school?"

"Well, yes, I'd love to," she said enthusiastically. "I always wanted to go on to graduate school, but then I got married and forgot about it."

"Then it seems to me that you *did* receive some excellent guidance after all."

Still doubtful, Susan wondered aloud, "Do you think so? Even if I felt that it was just my own voice talking?"

"Maybe it felt that way, but was it an idea or thought that you'd normally have, or was this something entirely different?"

"It was different, even surprising . . . which is why I thought I was making it up."

"That's the nature of guidance," I assured her. "It's so subtle and natural that you can miss it if you're not careful. It usually offers something different from the things that you normally think about. So, does the guidance you received appeal to you?"

"Yes," Susan said. "In fact, the more I consider it, the more sense it makes. I'm restless to grow in my own work and feel that I've postponed my dreams to be a good wife and mother instead of being myself, which is part of the reason I'm so unhappy. If it *is* my guide that's helping me, and not me making things up, then I feel very connected—and I'm ready to listen to more guidance."

As I told Susan, one key to success when making direct contact with our guides is to practice voicing aloud—without censoring—any inner guidance that we get. In the five-sensory, insensitive, world, we're conditioned to doubt ourselves and to surrender our lives to any external voice of authority. In the six-sensory world, our inner voice is the highest authority and prevails over any other. We must listen to it, respect it, voice it aloud, and honor what we feel without hesitation or apology.

And remember that your spirit guides' most important function is to connect with your soul and to make subtle suggestions . . . but they only do so when asked. By talking to your guides, you're simply sounding out your options, just as you'd bounce ideas off of a trusted confidant—and the more you speak to them, the more they respond to you.

When I was learning to connect with my guides, I often asked my teacher Charlie about the spirit world, and his response was always, "What do your guides say?"

Shy, and afraid of being wrong or sounding like a fool, I'd mumble, "I don't know."

He'd laugh and say, "Ask them."

Wrapped in his aura of love, humor, and safety, I'd tentatively go inward, peeking and poking around my heart for inspiration. Worried that it was my own voice, I'd nevertheless venture forth with an answer. The thrilling part was not the response, but the fact that I was sitting at the feet of a great authority figure, having him empower me to converse with my inner voice (and the voices of my guides) without having to feel fearful or defensive. At first it was awkward—even though I'd grown up in a spirit-filled world—but once I got the hang of it, it felt so real and authentic that there was no going back.

Did You Know That . . .

. . . when it comes to spirit guides, you're building a relationship with light beings who offer their help with love and friendship? Like all good friends, they always listen and reserve judgment, never try to control you or tell you what to do, and won't flatter you or cater to your ego.

Recently, I conducted a four-day workshop on connecting with guides, and in the class was a beautiful woman who was an M.D. and a practitioner of Ayurvedic medicine. When I asked the class to connect with their guides and ask questions, she said, "I don't think that these are my guides. I think it's all just me and that I'm very smart."

I asked her to step up to the podium and openly articulate her inner being. She boldly walked to the front of the room, but the minute she faced the audience she had a switch in her vibration and confidence. She suddenly looked like the proverbial deer caught in headlights, and she burst into tears at her own unexpected loss of confidence. She quickly discovered that choosing to connect, trust, and then express inner experience when one has been trained from day one to hide it can be deeply daunting.

Just as quickly as her tears came, they left, and a refreshed and relieved self emerged. It was then that I asked her to share what she asked her guides, and to give us only her "smart-self" answer.

"I asked them how I can be a better doctor and healer. Their answer was 'Be yourself.'"

"Is that your smart self answering?" I asked.

"I think so."

"Well, let's have more conversation to find out. Ask your inner self what being yourself means."

She did, and said, "Be honest, be loving, and be caring." After pausing for a moment, she added, "Share with people my intuitive capacities and ability to understand their wounds— especially around loss of love and support in the family—and let them know that I can use my ability to love and help them heal."

I observed that the vibration of these words was completely different: They were clear, simple, and real. The class nodded in agreement, and I asked her, "Is this your normal smart self or something else?"

She hesitated and then said, "No, this isn't my normal self. Maybe in the back of my heart I'd like to be like this, but as an M.D. it's too risky to be that personal with my patients. I'd usually never be so open and forward. I just try to let my patients know that I love them, but I'd *never* say so."

"Can you feel the difference between this communication and that of your normal smart self, even if they both enter your awareness in your own voice?" I asked.

She nodded and said, "If I were to really study this difference, I'd have to say that I've heard and ignored this other voice, and that it *does* feel like a guide. In fact, the more I listen to it out loud, the more it feels like my grandmother's voice that I knew as a child. She often told me that love heals. . . . Do you think that she could be my guide?"

"Ask," I said.

"Are you Grammy?" she asked, and then she smiled, for the voice had replied, "I am, and I'm glad that you're finally listening to me."

The class and I laughed because we felt truth in the vibration of her voice.

Your Turn

Whenever you're in doubt or in need of guidance, say aloud: "Let me ask my guides," and then do exactly that. Next, let them answer by saying, "They say [fill in the blank]." Don't worry that you're making things up—just listen to the content and vibration of the words that emerge as you let your inner being speak freely. Practice this for 10 to 15 minutes a day.

It's also very helpful to work with friends who are open and trustworthy, and who share your interest and desire to connect with guides. Take turns—first you, then your friend—asking the guides for insight, and then, with each of you as a witness to the other, sound out all that runs through your inner being, sorting out the different vibrations in the answer. The key is to be comfortable, enjoy the conversations, and treat them as normal and important. Try to have fun with this exercise and savor the process of exploration.

Connecting with your guides is the art of subtle communication, and the more that you practice sharing your *inner* world, the more comfortably it becomes a part of your *outer* world.

Chapter 10

A Step Further: Writing to Your Guides

In addition to talking to your guides, another direct way to communicate with them is through writing. Rather than articulating the messages that your guides give you vocally, you can write down your questions in a journal or notebook, and then receive their responses in writing. Guided writing works beautifully because it rests on the principle that we discussed earlier: Your hands are direct conduits to your heart—the place where your guides speak to you.

Getting Started

As you prepare to contact your guides, it's best to pick a specific time of day when you'll be relaxed and uninterrupted to write to them, and *write only then*. If you have questions or issues that come up before your writing session, jot them down in a small notebook and save them until your appointment. (Don't be surprised, however, if by writing time, the answers have appeared.) When it's time to get started, find a place where you can shut the door, unplug the phone, and ensure that you have privacy.

Notice that I said *privacy*, not *secrecy* . . . this is a very important point that I want to address because many clients have told me that they need to hide their efforts at contacting their spirit guides from those that are close to them because their spouse wouldn't approve, for example, or their family would judge them negatively. In contrast to privacy—which is a positive choice—secrecy implies shame, and if you try to contact your guides when feeling doubtful or secretive, you're at risk of attracting low-vibration entities (or guides who aren't very elevated and therefore don't have much to offer you), rather than high-vibration guides who can serve you.

Contacting your spirit guides is your right as a spiritual being, and you don't need another's approval when growing your own soul and seeking guided support to do so. If you're working to connect with your guides and are at risk of encountering negative reactions from others, it's self-loving and healthy to protect yourself and your efforts by keeping your pursuits discreet.

That being said, when you first sit down to begin guided writing, it's important that you state that it's your intention to work only with high-level spirit guides. One way to do this is to say a short prayer asking that your angels protect you and only allow high-vibration guides to enter your frequency as you write. You can also light a small votive candle to indicate the light of your spirit and to signal that you intend to only receive guidance that supports the highest good of your spirit.

The first question my students ask me is whether they should write to their guides by hand, or use a computer. Out of habit, I always used to say to write with a pen and paper (because it's more organic and bypasses the brain), but then I encountered people such as my husband, Patrick, who gets stressed when writing because he has terrible penmanship; or my daughter, who has dyslexia and gets confused when trying to write. They both find that working on a computer is much easier, so now—although I still advise people to write by hand if possible—I do suggest working on a computer if writing causes stress.

When writing to your guides by hand, you have two options: (1) Either use your dominant hand to write the question and your other hand to write the answer; or (2) mentally change channels and use your dominant hand for both. (Of course, if you use a computer, you'll type both your questions and your answers.) Your guides don't care which method you use, and they're going to show up when you ask them to, so just do what feels best—and keep in mind that the key is to write quickly and get into flow.

Once you've set your intention and are ready to start writing, introduce yourself and ask for guidance in this way: *I am* [your name] *and I am asking my spirit guides for assistance and support at this time.* Be polite and respectful, and remember that you're asking for guidance and not turning your life over for the spirit world to run. Word your questions appropriately, and avoid "Should I?" questions; instead simply ask: *What guidance can you offer on* [fill in the blank]?

Approach your guides gently and don't bombard them with too many questions at once. Stick to three or four at first, and don't get hung up on inquiries such as *Who are you?* because guides often respond by writing in groups. Just trust that you have summoned the highest guides to aid you in your writing exercise and leave it at that.

Keep your questions simple and direct. Your guides are intimately connected to you and are far more familiar with your struggles than you know, so there's no need for details. For example, you might write: *I'm struggling with finding satisfying work, and I feel blocked and frustrated. What guidance can you offer about the nature of my blocks, and what steps can I take to move forward?* (The guides are smart, so trust them to read between the lines.)

After you write your question, lift up your pen for a moment, open your heart, and turn your listening inward. Trust your body; relax; and then, holding the pen loosely, begin writing again when you feel the urge. Your guides will gently nudge you to write, so don't worry about your hand being "taken over." Although there were times when my guides were so enthusiastic and I was so open that it felt like a great force had taken over, usually (at least in the beginning) the urge to write is subtle, so when you feel it, begin. You may only get a few words, or you may get pages of guidance, depending on how receptive and calm you are. If you're genuinely open to insight and are willing to grow, a lot comes in.

When writing, you'll know that you're receiving guidance by the content—as subtle as it may be—because even when you write ideas that have crossed your mind, the vibration will resonate as support. On the other hand, if you receive guidance that makes you uncomfortable, throw it away or burn it, because a low-vibration entity may have slipped in and offered a useless opinion. Treat it like you would any bad advice—regardless of who it came from—and just ignore it.

To succeed at guided writing, be consistent but not obsessive. Check in with your guides once a day if you wish, but don't spend more than a half hour on this exercise. It's best to take guidance in small doses and then let it settle in. Savor it; think about it; assess if it leaves you calm, grounded, and uplifted; and then turn it over to your spirit for final analysis.

Did You Know That . . .

. . . when seeking guidance, you're not just looking for someone to agree with you? True high-level guides will support your soul's growth and inspire you, and if your requests are genuine, the channel will serve you well.

A client named Bernice used the pen-and-paper method to ask for guidance in her struggle with her weight. Her question was simple: *Why do I carry excess weight, and what can I do to shed it?* She then sat quietly, ready for information—and after 30 seconds, the urge to write kicked in, and the pen took off. She felt her guides transmitting answers so quickly that she could hardly keep up.

First Bernice wrote that in a past life she was a Polynesian princess and that her weight was a great source of power and pride; many of her people loved and respected her girth as a symbol of great prosperity. She wrote that she missed this special attention and wanted people to admire her again—which is why she's been reluctant to shed the excess pounds.

Next, she changed the channel, and the tone of her writing shifted. She wrote that her insulin levels were too high, and that a vegetarian diet and frequent meals would ground and calm her nervous system.

Her writing changed yet again, and she wrote that she'd been loved and celebrated for being a "good girl" throughout her childhood, and part of that praise was earned by being a good eater who cleaned her plate. She finished by writing that her weight would find proper balance when she stopped living for approval from others.

Reading what she wrote, Bernice marveled that the information had never crossed her mind before, but she felt that on a deep, organic level, it was right, and she used the information she received to make positive changes in her life. First, she had her insulin levels checked, and they were dangerously high—just as her guides had indicated. As for becoming a vegetarian, well, since my client was a Midwestern meat eater, she initially scoffed at such a notion, but because she was feeling so lethargic, she gave it a try . . . and over the next four months she dropped 53 pounds. And finally, in order to garner positive attention for something other than eating, she joined a choir at her church, where her beautiful voice earned her the opportunity to sing solos that really showcased her talent.

When I asked Bernice what her feelings were on the subject of past lives, she replied, "Well, who knows? I'm losing weight, so I won't question it!"

Similarly, my client Tim learned that there is no limit to the guidance that can be received through guided writing when, within weeks of starting, he found himself writing the novel he'd long struggled with.

Another client, Mitch, asked his guides for advice on his love life, and the written response was *sandwich shop*—which he dismissed as absurd and threw away. Three weeks later, his buddy at work said, "Want to grab some lunch? There's a new sandwich shop two blocks from here that just opened up." Making no connection, Mitch walked in and was immediately smitten by the cashier—and she seemed equally interested.

They flirted, and as she handed him his lunch, she said, "We close at five, if you're free in the evening." They set a date to meet for a drink, and it didn't occur to Mitch that he was guided there until their third date. That night, just as he was drifting off to sleep, he suddenly remembered what he'd written, and he immediately apologized and thanked his guides for their guidance.

Your Turn

When writing to your guides, it's important that you relax . . . and don't worry that you won't make contact. They *will* write back, but it may take a few minutes—or longer. In fact, it may even take a writing session or two before you hear back from them. Just try to be patient. . . . They'll respond!

To practice writing to your guides, simply follow the steps below:

- **Step #1:** Work in a quiet, uninterrupted space; and before you begin, light a small votive candle and say a short prayer for protection from low-level energies.

- **Step #2:** State your intention by writing, *I seek to converse only with guides of the highest vibration.* Next introduce yourself by writing, *I'm* [your name] *and I'm asking for assistance at this time.*

- **Step #3:** Proceed to write your questions, one at a time, and then lift your pen and relax.

- **Step #4:** Hold your pen still but loosely in your hand and be ready to have the guides take over and respond to your questions by writing back. Expect ideas from your guides to flow into your mind and then onto the paper. Don't allow your mind to censor what you write or trick you into believing it's just you making things up—remember that guidance is subtle and will feel natural. When the flow stops, put the pen down and reread what you've written.

As a final note, I suggest that you keep all of your writings in the same journal or notebook and don't discard any of them (unless, of course, they leave you feeling uncomfortable, in which case, burn them). The guidance you receive may not be what you expect or want, or you may not understand it immediately, but you should keep it anyway. You see, in my experience, most guidance makes sense in time—if not right away—so a good rule of thumb is to set your writing aside and refer to it later. If that doesn't work, ask your guides for more information at another writing session, and then, if it *still* isn't clear, let it go.

Chapter 11

Learning to See Your Spirit Guides

Seeing your guides is perhaps the most challenging way of connecting with them, since they exist on an entirely different, nonphysical vibrational plane, and it takes a tremendous amount of effort for them to modify their frequency so that you can see them. At the same time, your own frequency must rise to a certain level in order to activate what is known as your "third eye" (the inner eye you imagine with), which you use to see your guides.

People who have a very active and developed inner eye are most likely to see their guides quickly. If you aren't a person who finds it easy to visualize in pictures, don't worry. We all have an inner eye, and it worked quite well when we were young—in fact, it's the reason why so many children are able to see guides and angels . . . although they're usually referred to as "imaginary friends." Sadly, when we begin to attend school, we're conditioned to stop using our inner eye; instead, we're encouraged to turn our focus outward for direction, which gradually disconnects us from our ability to see the spirit world.

The good news is that with a little effort and some good old-fashioned patience and practice, you can reactivate this natural channel to the spirit world and begin to actually "see" your guides. In preparation for contacting your spirit guides, try the following exercises to help you reopen your inner eye:

Exercise #1: Learn to Be in the Here-and-Now

First, look closely at your surroundings and notice every detail you can about what's right in front of your face. This may sound contradictory: Why concentrate on physical reality when you're trying to see the spirit plane? Well, most people are so caught up with replays of the past or imaginings of the future that they don't focus on the present; consequently, they end up missing out on the here-and-now.

Seeing your guides is the hyperacute ability to focus on what's going on right in front of you—only in another dimension. To develop this ability, you need to practice seeing everything around you, which will stimulate your dormant inner eye and get it working again.

Exercise #2: Take the Time to Daydream

If your life is overly hectic or you work with a very tight schedule, it's going to be a real challenge to connect with your guides through daydreaming, because it requires a greater investment of time and focus than connecting with them telepathically. However, if you're willing to give it the extra effort, you'll succeed.

As children, we all participated in "woolgathering," and in doing so, we often left our bodies and connected to (and even played with) our spirit guides. The most debilitating instruction we ever received as children was to "stop daydreaming!" And when we did, we disconnected from the healers, angels, and spirit friends who were helping us.

Letting your mind wander frees up your focus from the linear, physical plane and expands and trains your inner eye to see beyond it. When I was being taught by my teacher Charlie to see guides, he continually told me that physical appearance is the least accurate representation of any being, and he encouraged me to look past it and deeper into people and things. Once you train yourself to do so, and to look into the essence of things—including yourself—it only takes a small leap to begin seeing your guides directly.

Before you begin this exercise, make sure that you're in a grounded, unemotional state. If you're upset, you can first call on the ministry of angels to calm and settle you, and then you can begin (but limit yourself to 10 to 15 minutes a day). You don't need to go to a particular place for this exercise— you can do it on the bus, on the train, or in the car (as long as you're not driving!); or while you're cooking dinner, doing the dishes, or mowing the lawn. No matter where you are,

try to imagine what your spirit looks, feels, and sounds like
. . . and think about what makes it happy. Work to see it in
three dimensions and in color, imagining everything about
how you're seeing your spirit with your inner eye in as much
detail as you can.

After practicing that for a while, try to see the spirit of
your loved ones in your mind's eye—imagine those of your
children, parents, partner, and even your animals. Don't
rush; instead, let yourself enjoy this exercise for several weeks.
It will work out your inner eye, raise your vibration, and train
you to look past physical appearances and tune in to high
frequencies all at once.

I had a client named Sarah who imagined seeing her spirit
for several weeks, and every time she saw it she imagined
herself riding a beautiful chestnut horse at full gallop across
the countryside, with her hair flowing wildly in the wind. (The
scene was a far cry from her job as an intake administrator at
a city hospital!) She began to feel that the horse itself was her
guide, and with each daydream she focused less and less on
being on the horse, and more and more on where the horse
was taking her. Several weeks of daydreaming eventually led
them both to Provo, Utah.

Sarah, who lived in Cleveland, knew nothing about Provo
and thought that it was silly to have her horse take her there.
She kept an open mind about it, however, and you can imagine
her surprise when, ten months later, she was introduced to a
chiropractor named Fred—who was from Provo—at a health-
care conference. He told her that he was starting the first
alternative health-care center in the Cleveland area, and after

a fairly brief conversation, asked if she'd be interested in taking a wild ride and managing the center for him.

My client's daydream began to make sense, and she accepted his offer, beginning the professional adventure of her life! And to remind her of how she got there, she placed a small bronze horse on her desk.

Sarah was able to master this exercise because she was willing to take the steps that everyone must in order to successfully see their guides: (1) They need to want to see them; (2) they have to believe that they will; and (3) they must accept what they see. Not all guides take the form of a human, physical body, so if that's what's expected, the exercise is likely to be disappointing.

When I initially tried to see my guides, for instance, the first one appeared as a bright blue dot hovering above my bed. My sister Cuky sees one of her guides—my deceased aunt Emma—not as she looked in life, but as a pool of water that appears in the corner of her bedroom. And when a client named Marvin began to work very sincerely on seeing his guides, he only saw clouds of white feathers, as though a down pillow had exploded. He accepted that this was his guide and named it "White Feathers."

Similarly, my client Dahlia originally saw her guide as a light blue heron that sat across from her and conveyed messages to her telepathically. The blue heron eventually morphed into a beautiful light blue being, whose name (my client learned telepathically) was Erin. Sometimes she sees the heron, and sometimes she sees Erin . . . it's always a surprise.

Eventually Dahlia noticed that the heron usually appears when she's in a mental rut—its appearance means that she needs to lighten up to receive new ideas. When Erin appears, she gets specific instructions, not just a message to change her mood or perspective. Regardless of the changes in the way her guide appears, what Dahlia sees is always perfect according to her need at the time.

Remember, spirit *does* have a way of revealing itself to you—it's up to you to learn to see it.

Did You Know That . . .

. . . guides like to be efficient? They'll appear and connect by giving a short specific message.

. . . the highest guides tend to be clear, simple, and bright, and leave you with a light feeling?

. . . it's best to be consistent and connect with your guides at the same time every day because they'll treat your attention as an appointment with them and make an effort to show up on time?

. . . appointing a specific time of day to pull back the veil and see beyond the physical world trains your subconscious mind to filter the spiritual world less stringently?

When you're ready to see your guides, sit in a relaxing chair or lie down on your bed, close your physical eyes, and imagine an interior movie screen lighting up in your mind. Ask your spirit to project itself onto the screen, and then relax and get ready to enjoy the show. If your mind has a hard time settling down, or your body feels restless, imagine your spirits sitting down next to you, as if you were in a movie theater and you invited them to watch the screen with you.

Next, ask your spirit to project the most beautiful place in the world onto the screen—a place where you can connect with your guides anytime you wish. Then, breathing comfortably in through your nose and out through your mouth, allow whatever pops up to appear on the screen. Try to be patient and accept whatever appears without resistance.

Perhaps what you see in your mind's eye will be familiar—it may be a favorite spot from childhood, or a place you traveled to in the past and enjoyed—yet it could also be a place you've never seen before. Even if it makes no sense, your guides choose the way they want to appear and will select the images that work best for your connection.

For example, Thomas's childhood kitchen appeared on his inner screen . . . with a babbling brook running right through the middle of it. When he asked his guide to appear, she popped out of the brook, sat at the kitchen table, and then dove back in. Perplexed at first, it later occurred to Thomas that his favorite memories from childhood were of baking cookies with his mom in the kitchen, and of fishing in a small stream with his dad. Having these scenes converge in his imagination as the perfect place to meet his guide was something he never would have thought of on his own.

If you find that nothing appears on your screen, don't worry—your inner eye may simply be a little slower to activate than you'd like. In that case, it's okay to help it along a little. If nothing appears, invite your spirit to decorate your meeting place in any way you'd like, and do your best to choose the perfect spot. Once you've done so, remember to close your eyes and ask that only the highest, most helpful guides appear there to take a seat across from you.

Be patient, as you may need to do this several times before you have success—however, if you persist, your guides will appear. Accept what comes when they do, and remember that guides don't necessarily take a human form. They may come as symbols, and don't be surprised if they also appear in different forms at different times.

Monique, one of my clients, bemoaned her inactive inner eye, but it lit right up when she was invited to decorate her inner sanctum on her own. She chose to meet her guide in a cozy, oak-paneled room with a crackling fireplace; two thick armchairs in plaid, velvet fabric; and floor-to-ceiling bookcases filled with tomes that contained the answers to every question in the Universe. At her feet were an antique red and gold oriental rug; two thick, leather footstools; and a large, sleeping, yellow Labrador retriever. There were standing lamps behind the chairs with colorful, lead-glass shades, and a ten-foot-tall, floor-to-ceiling, oak door that was closed shut to the outside world to give them privacy.

When she asked to see her guide, instead of a person appearing, a book flew off a shelf and opened on the footstool. Accepting it, she then asked her guide about her husband's mental health, since she suspected that he was developing dementia. In response, another volume flew off the bookcase and when it opened, the word *chelation* (defined as a process for removing metals and toxins from the body) appeared in her mind's eye.

In response to the message, Monique took her husband to be tested for toxicity, and they discovered that he had very high levels of mercury in his body—a condition that can mimic early dementia. Later, she happily reported to me that, soon after undergoing chelation therapy, his health began to slowly improve.

Your Turn

Let's review the things that you can do on a daily basis to start training your inner eye to see your spirit guides. Remember that you only need 10 to 15 minutes each day for these exercises—after all, you don't want to wear out your inner eye!

- Start paying close attention to what's in the here-and-now.

- Return to your childhood pastime of daydreaming to activate your inner eye by imagining what your spirit guides and the guides of others might look like.

- Keep your eyes relaxed and almost closed, and let your inner eye do the "looking."

- Accept whatever comes to mind, even if it makes no sense at first. Be patient—in time it will.

Now that you've opened the channel that allows you to directly connect with your spirit guides, let's move on and meet them individually.

PART IV

Introducing Your Spirit Guides

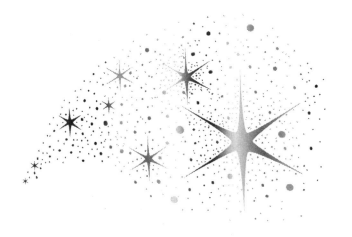

Chapter 12

The Spirit Guides of the Nature Kingdom

Now that you've opened yourself up to receiving spiritual guidance and practiced some basic techniques for communicating with your guides, it's time to meet some of the different spiritual beings you may be hearing from. As you become more attuned to the spirit in all things, the first guides you may sense are the forces of nature.

Grouped together, the nature spirits are called elementals. Comprised of the spirits of earth, water, fire, and air, they're sometimes known as *gnomes, sprites, sylphs, devas,* and *salamanders* (which are not anything like the small reptilian creatures). Although this may sound like the stuff of fairy tales, every living thing has its own spirit force and vibration that looks after it.

The nature spirits are wonderfully therapeutic, and by raising your sensitivity to their presence and asking for their help, you'll immediately begin to feel their support. When you learn to identify them and become open to receiving their gifts, the natural world will then become a place of healing and excitement for you.

The Earth Spirits

It's best to start connecting with this spirit realm by concentrating on the spirits of the earth—also known as devas—beginning with the trees, flowers, and of course, Mother Earth herself. The earth is an incredible living, breathing spirit, majestically supporting all of the life on this planet. Affectionately known as Gaia, she is the organic mother of us all, and becoming sensitive to her energy instantly helps us feel physically stronger and supported.

Connecting with the earth is known as "getting grounded"—a term that's casually tossed about, but rarely fully understood to be the act of allowing our spirit to be nurtured by Mother Earth. When we're disconnected from her we feel scattered, weak, easily pushed around by life, and cut off from support. By raising our sensitivity to and becoming conscious of her, our life calms down and our basic sense of security kicks in.

Not one of us is so smart that we can live without Gaia's force beneath us . . . even concrete cannot fully block her energy. If you ever doubt her power, just conjure up the magnitude of a big earthquake to bring you back to reality. At the same time, she can also be astonishingly gentle— nothing is so restorative to your body and bones as a massage from her.

About a dozen years ago, my husband, Patrick, and I took our daughters to Hawaii for the first time. When Sonia hit the beach, she could hardly contain herself. It felt so delicious and soothing to that five-year-old that she threw herself onto the sand; grabbed it by the handful; squeezed, smelled, and even tried to eat it. She rolled around in the wet sand for hours and never tired of it. As I was putting her to bed that evening, her heart was so brimming with joy that she gave me a full-body hug and said, "Mom, before today I used to love you like a dot . . . now I love you like a circle."

If you feel drained, disconnected, unsupported, and unloved, tap in to Mother Earth's spirit and let it nurture you. Have your spirit ask her to enfold you with her endless arms and pull you back to her breast. Gaia's spirit is so powerful that connecting to her will lift depression and fear, and can even ease one of our greatest social diseases—chronic fatigue syndrome.

Patrick goes so far as to incorporate the healing energy of Mother Earth into his work as a therapeutic massage therapist. One of his practices is to simply hold his client's feet at the end of every massage and let Gaia's healing life force enter his or her body, filling it with her vitality and power. He does this for several minutes, saying nothing—just allowing the earth spirit to do the work. Many of his clients report that at this point in their session, they fall into a state of profound relaxation and feel as if they're plugged in to a generator that is restoring every cell in their body.

Hot-stone massage therapy, another recently popularized treatment, channels the earth spirit in the same way. The spirit in the rocks, which are strategically placed over a person's body, manages to touch bone marrow and has the power to calm, fortify, and restore strength to the individual like nothing else.

By the same token, the spirits in flowers work to calm and balance your emotional body—the first layer of energy overlaying your physical body—which goes through a lot of wear and tear in a day, a week, or a lifetime. It can get weak, thin, and torn, leaving you prey to all kinds of emotional and psychic distress.

Tapping in to the spirit of flowers doesn't take too much effort . . . simply smell a rose, appreciate an orchid, or sniff a sachet of lavender to see what I mean. If you're feeling flat, weak, or uninspired, bringing your subtle awareness forward to connect with the flower and plant fairies will restore your balance, and can gently calm and reweave the emotional body and restore balance.

Some people have become so connected to the spiritual energies in flowers and their immense capacity to heal the emotional body that there are entire alternative-healing methods devoted to the therapeutic qualities of flower essences. To give yourself an added boost, you can even look into using these essences, which embody the restorative spirit of plants and flowers, and are available in health-food stores as well as on the Internet. Each specific plant extract brings a different result by tapping in to the particular energy you are focusing on. For example, holly relieves you of being critical, lavender opens and calms the heart, and violet builds confidence.

Perhaps the most remarkable example of the power of working with plant and flower fairies can be found in a community called Findhorn in northern Scotland. By paying close attention to the nature spirits and celebrating and revering their world, this experimental community has been able to grow huge vegetables, plants, and flowers in soil devoid of proper nutrients. Although no one quite knows *who* connects with and honors the fairies at Findhorn, its inhabitants are regularly rewarded with huge gardens.

You, too, can really connect with fairies if you grow a garden—even if you just nurture a few potted plants. The next time that you find yourself mindlessly watering the azaleas, stop and feel their energy and appreciate their strong, yet gentle, spirit. Talk to your plants and flowers and even play classical music for them . . . after all, experiments have proven that their spirits react to kindness and in response, they'll go wild and grow like crazy.

If you *really* want to feel some psychic support, take this a step further and hug a tree. I'm completely serious when I say this. We (especially those of us in the Western world) have become lazy and dull in our subtle awareness, but very few people can remain immune to the formidable grounding and healing power of a tree. Be willing to look as loony as a lark if you must, but take the risk and throw your arms around the next oak or elm in your path. Place your heart up against the bark and see how you feel. If that's just too over the top and you can't bring yourself to enjoy that experience, at least plop down at the foot of a tree and connect with its majesty through its roots.

The spirits of trees are so powerful that they act like amplifiers for your psychic sensibilities. Connecting with their energy will pull your awareness deep into the spirit world, quickly enhancing your ability to connect with higher-frequency entities, such as your guides and angels. And although it may not happen overnight, if you work with trees for a few weeks, you'll no doubt start attuning to other spirit forces.

If you're a city dweller, you may have to use a little extra effort to attune to the earth spirits, but quite honestly, the benefits and rewards are worth it. City life is very stressful and draining, so connecting with the nature spirits is all the more urgent. In the end, you'll become calmer, more grounded, and emotionally more peaceful.

The Water Spirits

In addition to Gaia and the earth devas, you can also begin to access the spirits of water. The Bible itself contains several references to its power, and one of the most exciting books I've read recently is *The Hidden Messages in Water* by Masaru Emoto. In it, the author not only explores, but actually photographs, water spirits and the responses they have to energy. He shows that when water is exposed to angry, ugly energy, it will form dark, misshapen crystals. On the other hand, when exposed to loving, kind thoughts, it forms gorgeous crystal patterns, showing that water is alive with consciousness and responsive to our thoughts and attitudes.

The water spirits are powerful and cleansing, and they work to wash away the old and outworn. They can be ferocious when necessary—as the horrified world witnessed in the tsunami of Christmas 2004, when the force of the water literally wiped multitudes of people off the face of the earth in a matter of minutes. At the same time, this very same force indirectly united the world in loving cooperation to help those who survived.

The world's awareness is beginning to be heightened in regard to the power of water spirits by the increasing frequency of water-related natural disasters in general, such as recent hurricanes, floods, and the aforementioned tsunami. Global water shortages and droughts (even our current fascination with designer water) are also bringing the world's attention to the influence water spirits have on our daily existence.

Interestingly enough, people connect most frequently with water spirits in dreams, claiming that some of their most disturbing, or refreshing, dreams involve water lore. For instance, every time my sister dreams of water, it's a warning that some decision she's made (or is considering making) isn't sound and must be reversed or refused. I also have a client who dreamed of drowning in a sudden flood, only to be suddenly laid off from her job three days later. In both cases, the message that was delivered through the water theme was that each of them had something they needed to let go of.

Connecting to the water spirits refreshes your perspective and can keep you from becoming stuck in a neutral rut, as anyone who has enjoyed a walk on the beach can attest.

There are several ways to benefit from the cleansing and relaxing power of water. For example, you can install a small fountain in your home and invite it to refresh all of the energies dwelling there. I've seen fountains costing as little as $14 at Wal-Mart and Target, and the fact that they're no longer a pricey item for the privileged indicates the growth of mainstream sensitivity to the healing power of the water spirits.

Another good way to connect is to carry a small spray bottle with fresh water and blast yourself throughout the day, especially when you've experienced a challenging moment or fall into a mood of self-doubt. The water spirits will work on your behalf to keep such negativity or doubt from settling in, and will help restore your energy to balance.

The Air Spirits

The air spirits, which can be felt in gentle breezes, as well as fierce tornadoes, are of the neutral plane. That means that when you connect with them, you energize, calm, and clear your mind and soul. The first, and perhaps most important connection happens when you simply take a deep breath— when you do, the air spirits enter and interact with your own spirits and bring you into the moment, stimulating your mind, improving your ability to focus, and allowing you to feel subtle energies.

On the other hand, when you hold your breath, you disconnect from the air spirits, stifle your own spirit, and cut yourself off from the flow of life. One of the best psychic practices for inviting in the support of the air spirits is to begin each day with a series of five to ten deep, cleansing breaths before you even get out of bed. As you breathe, ask the air spirits to clear your mind, refresh your blood, invigorate your organs, and help you greet life that day with enthusiasm and clarity.

Connecting with the air spirits—the sylphs—is also a very smart practice whenever you find yourself feeling fearful or anxious. Stop, breathe, and relax; breathe and relax; breathe and relax—with practice, this quick exercise will calm you immediately and cleanse your thoughts.

It's important to connect with the air devas when facing major decisions, undergoing interviews, negotiating with others, or giving speeches. They help to prevent your mind from becoming muddy or confused, to keep your thoughts flowing, and to tune you in to the refined frequencies of your other spirit guides. Since they're also the gatekeepers of telepathy, they provide the access line to all other entities within the spirit community.

Did You Know That . . .

. . . earth spirits are also known as *gnomes, fairies, tree devas,* or *elves,* and that they provide grounding and attend to emotional healing?

. . . water spirits are called *naiads, sea nymphs, undines,* or *sprites,* and that they're responsible for the cleansing, refreshing, and clearing of our spirits?

. . . air spirits are sometimes referred to as *air devas, builders, zephyrs,* or *sylphs,* and that they can be called upon to calm us and to help with focus and mental clarification?

. . . fire spirits are known by metaphysicians as *salamanders,* and that they inspire passion, new life, blessings, creativity, and spiritual healing?

The Fire Spirits

The last of the nature spirits are the salamanders—the dancing energies that spark, crackle, and mesmerize all at once. The fire spirits excite our passion and creativity, and connecting with them helps raise our sense of can-do-ism and our eternal youth. Fire spirits need to be called in when we've lost our luster, or when we find ourselves in a mental quagmire of blame, excuses, or self-pity. . . . There's nothing like a good salamander to shake us free of a habitual funk.

Have you ever observed how gazing into a fire evokes timelessness and romance—not just for lovers, but for life itself? When connecting to the fire spirits, see what wakes up in your own spirit . . . what forgotten dreams, desires, and passions come alive? This is the healing dance between the fire's spirit and yours.

On the other hand, the fire spirits also surprise, shock, and if necessary, clear the slate. I've witnessed more than a few of them burn a person's home or business to the ground, leaving those involved instantly reduced to a *tabula rasa*.

When you call the fire spirits forward, be attentive to their dance, their crackle, and their frenzy. Salamanders ask you to step lightly, be flexible and inventive, adapt, and respond. It's best to be the student when calling on them, and to *never* take them for granted.

To connect with them, light a fire, but know that you must remain with the fire until it's gone out, been put out, or has burned down to embers, because fire spirits like to be watched. If you ignore them by walking away from a fire, they may get your attention by burning the place down!

Besides the salamanders, fire also invokes the greatest of all spirit guides—the Holy Spirit—as fire symbolizes the Divine spark that gives life to all of us, which is represented by the eternal flame. (This is why virtually every religion utilizes some aspect of fire in their symbolism and ceremonies.)

Calling on the Holy Spirit to revitalize and heal your spirit is one of the most powerful requests you can make. In fact, when I was growing up and attending Catholic school, I went regularly to mass, and I loved the ritual of lighting candles to call up the Holy Spirit and the Holy Family to burn brightly in my heart and to watch over me. (You can do this by lighting perpetual candles as well, which are available in the Mexican-food section of most supermarkets and in most churches.) This weekly fire ritual kept me feeling connected to God and the Holy Spirit and helped the fire burn brighter within me.

Your Turn

The best part of connecting to the nature spirits is that you begin to sense how wonderfully supported you are and how much your spirit is a part of the many levels of spirit all around. They're eager to serve, to please, to inspire, and to support, and will do all this if you give them due respect and reverence. Just know that they're there and they'll bring you many beautiful gifts—and don't forget to enjoy them.

Connect in some way with the earth, water, air, and fire spirits at least once a day to keep you healthy and your life force balanced. Try these simple exercises to get you started:

— Perhaps the best way to connect with the earth spirits is to stop whatever you're doing right now and look (or better yet, go) outside. If you're lucky enough to be in a natural setting, sit quietly and focus on the buzz of life sprouting forth from the ground. It's even more effective to actually lie down on the earth, on top of a blanket if you'd like, and breathe in her spirit through every pore.

If you live in the city, go to the nearest patch of green to make your connection.

— Raise your awareness of the water spirits when you shower or bathe by asking them to help you renew from and release outworn energies. Appreciate their healing properties and ask them to clear your body, mind, and aura of all negativity and psychic debris.

— A powerful way to call the air spirits is to breathe in through your nose slowly, then, thumping your palm on your heart, exhale with full force while saying a loud "Ha!" This activates your spirit, opens telepathic channels, and shoos away all negative mind chatter occupying your brain. It's a great quick fix to get you instantly realigned with your spirit and brings your full attention to the moment.

— A safe way to ask fire spirits to bring spice, passion, and creative excitement to your life is by burning candles, lighting incense, or building a fire in your hearth. Ask the fire spirits to wake your courage and potential, and to keep you from falling asleep at the wheel of your life or forgetting who you are. And remember: If you burn candles, watch over them; if you use a fireplace, check the flue and safety doors; and if you burn perpetual candles, place them in a sink or bathtub when you leave the house. These wise precautions simply reflect a healthy respect for the spirit and power of fire.

Chapter 13

Your Runners

Recently I was talking about a group of spirit guides known as "runners" with my friend Greg as my husband and I drove with Greg and his wife to a reception in downtown Chicago. It was a cold, rainy Friday during rush hour, and I was telling my friend how much easier life is when I call on my runners for help. He snorted in disbelief and challenged me, saying, "Well, call them for a parking spot, then! And make sure that it's close to the reception so that we don't have to walk or pay for a garage."

No sooner were the words out of his mouth when a car pulled out from a metered spot directly across from where the reception was being held.

"See what I mean," I said. "And better yet, it's one of those meters that we don't have to pay on since it's past six o'clock!"

When the reception was over, Greg once again tested me: "Okay, parking meters are easy," he said. "Let's see what your runners can do about finding a table for four at a good restaurant on a Friday night without waiting. . . . Now *that* will make a believer out of me."

"Where would you like to try?" I asked.

He chose an extremely popular French bistro called La Sardine, which is across the street from Oprah Winfrey's Harpo Studios. "Usually they're packed, but since we're close, let's give it a try," I said.

We approached the restaurant, and sure enough, the house was packed.

"Table for four," I said.

The hostess asked if we had a reservation, and just as I said, "No," her phone rang. After taking the call, she turned to me, smiled, and said, "You're in luck—a party of four just cancelled."

And that was just the beginning, as the runners were working overtime that night. As a delightful topper to the evening, our waiter showed up with beautiful desserts. Not having ordered them, we sent them back, only to have them returned. "A gift on the house," he said. In one night, my runners made a believer out of Greg, and sprinkled magic throughout our entire evening.

Who Are Your Runners?

These are handy guides for all situations, and the first ones you may want to invoke for help. My teacher Charlie taught me to call them "runners" because that's exactly what they do: run ahead and help you find things that you've lost or misplaced; or connect you to things that you seek, such as apartments, items on sale, or even parking spaces.

Runners are spirits who are very close to the earth and the natural world, and are usually indigenous souls who once inhabited the area where you reside today. For example, people living in America will often have Native American runners, since they're connected to the territory where you are (not to your ancestral roots). Similarly, you can be African American living in England or Scotland and have a Celtic runner, or you can be a Chinese Australian living in New Zealand and have a Maori runner. A runner's loyalties are with the land, not with you.

What these guides do best is sprinkle magic on your life. You see, the more magic you feel, the more you open your heart; and the more open your heart, the better your vibration and the happier your spirit. When your soul is delighted, everyone you meet feels it, too. That's why the runners' work is so important—it keeps us believing in the goodness of life and of our world.

I've invoked my runners for more than 30 years, and they've never let me down. And sometimes they even help me find things I didn't know I'd lost! For instance, one morning last week, after a night of working late in my office catching up on paperwork, I had an overwhelming urge to look through the wastebasket before my assistant arrived and emptied it. I grabbed a handful of papers I'd tossed in the night before and found an envelope containing two weeks' worth of bank deposits, which I'd forgotten to drop off the day before. If not for my runners, I would have been seriously out of luck.

On another occasion many years ago when I was a flight attendant, my runners saved me from what could have been a job-threatening situation. At that time, I had to commute twice a week from Chicago (which was where I lived) to St. Louis (where I was based)—all at my own expense. This was costly, even with my employee discount, and tricky, as the Chicago–St. Louis flights were always full. If I missed a flight, I could have lost my job. So, during those years I depended heavily on my runners to save me a seat on a flight so I could arrive in St Louis without any trouble.

On this particular day, my runners led me away from my flight ten minutes before departure, even though I'd already been assigned a seat, and the new flight would cost $50 more. I didn't know what they were up to, but I turned in my boarding pass and signed up for the other flight. I got on board, and 40 minutes later, I arrived in St. Louis.

Not seeing friends who were on the flight I'd abandoned, I looked at the arrival board and saw that it had been cancelled. I asked the agent what had happened, and he said that they'd found a mechanical problem right before departure. None of my colleagues on that flight made it to work that day—but I did, of course, with the help of my runners.

Runners rarely communicate with words; instead, they just nudge you without your necessarily knowing why. When I felt compelled to check the wastebasket or change my flight, I simply acted without thinking. My runners didn't run through my brain with an explanation—they just grabbed me and pulled me in the direction I needed to go.

Your runners are always watching out for you, and they're there to help you as soon as you take the time to ask.

My friend Ella lost an heirloom necklace her grandmother had given her shortly before she died. Not believing in her vibes or her guides, she called me and asked if I could help her. Normally I would have tried, but my vibes insisted that I give the assignment back to her. "Not this time, Ella," I said. "My vibes say that you should send your runners to look for it."

"You know I don't believe in all that," she whined. "Can't you please help me find it?"

"No, I can't. But if you ask nicely, your runners might." I advised her to ask politely, because runners are a touchy bunch. They're great scouts and detectives, since they're so closely connected to the area—but they tend to be proud, so you must appeal to them respectfully and not boss them around.

Ella moaned in protest, but she eventually gave it a try. "Please help me locate my grandmother's necklace," she pleaded, sitting defeated on the sofa after exhausting every hiding spot she could think of.

Ten minutes later she got up, and without thinking, opened her sock drawer and fumbled around, not knowing why. Suddenly she felt a lumpy sock, stuck her hand into it, and found the necklace. *How on earth did it get there?* she wondered. Then she remembered that she'd asked her husband to hide it just before they went on a weekend trip several months earlier, since she'd just received it and wasn't comfortable leaving it in her jewelry box. He'd buried it in the sock drawer, and they'd both forgotten about it. . . . But the runners didn't—they watched him hide the necklace, and took Ella right to it once she asked politely for their help.

You can ask your runners to help you find just about anything, including a parking space. Charlie taught me this trick years ago: He told me to send my runners ahead to save me a great parking spot every time I got into the car—and not just any spot, mind you, but the *best* spot—if I asked politely.

I taught my friend Debra about runners and parking spaces years ago, and she's embraced their existence completely. She first turns on the ignition, envisions where she's headed and what kind of parking spot she desires, and then she asks her runners to secure it for her.

One day she invited me to lunch, and as we approached the restaurant, the sky blackened and suddenly unleashed a torrential spring downpour. "No problem," she said. "I'll send my runners to get us a good parking spot so we won't get soaked."

Sure enough, as she drove into the restaurant's parking lot, a car that was parked about 20 feet from the door pulled out, leaving a great spot for us.

"That's my runners for you," she said.

No sooner had she said that when another car parked only *ten* feet from the entrance pulled out. I turned to her and said, "Now that's *my* runners for you!"

We both squealed with delight as we enjoyed our "dry" lunch.

Did You Know That . . .

. . . runners save time, frustration, and confusion, and help alleviate sadness resulting from loss? Appreciate them generously for serving you well, and they'll work twice as hard the next time.

Runners come in all shapes, sizes, and colors, but they do have three things in common: (1) They're quick and waste no time helping when asked; (2) they're strongly connected to the earth and nature and come from past lives, where they were natural scouts; and (3) they don't speak—they just act if you ask politely.

Not only do runners find lost things, save seats on planes, and turn up parking spaces, they help you locate items that you need but can't quite get your hands on. This was true for my client Myrna, who has size 11 feet and could never find stylish shoes in her size. Used to having sales clerks roll their eyes at her and make rude comments about her feet, she nearly gave up until she discovered runners (who she now has a very deep affection for) in one of my classes.

The first time she asked her runners to help, she was led to a new store in the mall where she found a pair of beautiful black leather boots that she loved. Hopeful, but used to disappointment, she asked the salesman if they came in size 11.

"Well, normally they don't," he replied, "but just today I received two pairs of 11s."

As she tried on the boots, which fit her perfectly, Myrna chatted with the salesman and discovered that he understood her frustration, since his wife also had size 11 feet. Consequently, he said that he'd found every designer and shoe store in the area that carried size 11s, and even knew when they arrived. He gave her the store list along with the boots, all but ending Myrna's 20 years of shoe misery and low self-esteem resulting from her big feet.

Runners know how difficult it is to accomplish all that we want to in a lifetime, and they're wonderful assistants to keep us from wasting time and energy. They can be generous and indulgent as they work, too.

For instance, a client named Steven was running late for his flight from Denver to New York, was caught in long security lines, and was certain that he'd miss his plane. Sending his runners ahead, he rushed to the gate and was told that the flight was closed and it was too late to board. Just then, another agent walked off the jetway toward the podium. Seeing Steven, he said, "The bags aren't fully loaded yet, so we can put him on."

Together, they ran down the jetway and knocked on the plane door. Steven then boarded the flight—where he was led to a seat in first class! So, not only did his runners come through by getting him on the flight, they upgraded him as well.

Your Turn

Working with your runners is very easy: All you need to do is ask for their help—and remember that they respond best if you speak to them in a soft rather than an agitated tone. (And be very respectful when you invoke them by saying "Please" instead of giving them an order.) Once you've asked for what you need, you should relax, sit back, and stop thinking about it for at least 20 minutes. The moment you shut your brain off, the runners will move in and get you going in the right direction.

One of my teachers once said, "If you stop and think, the moment is lost." This couldn't be more true, since in order to work with your runners, you must be willing to follow your instincts without hesitation and be flexible.

Finally, it's very important to keep in mind that runners appreciate recognition. Yes, they take great satisfaction in serving well and love to be asked . . . but they also love to be thanked.

Chapter 14

Your Helpers

A friend of mine named Natalie became very interested in her family's history several years ago, and it became her nearly full-time hobby to find out all she could about her relatives, past and present. She began to piece together the clan's genealogy, but ran into a dead end when an estranged uncle wouldn't share any of his information with her. This frustrated Natalie, but she wasn't deterred.

One day she was relaxing in her living room when she suddenly felt the presence of her deceased father whoosh down and pass before her eyes. The feeling was so strong that it compelled Natalie to get up out of her chair, walk directly over to her computer, and Google her father's name— something she'd never done before (or even thought about, for that matter). She began scrolling through the 106 pages that came up, but none of the data applied to her family.

Not wanting to waste her time sifting through this mountain of information—and not quite sure what she was looking for in the first place—my friend arbitrarily decided that she'd only look at page 16, and if there was nothing relevant to her family there, she'd stop. Expecting to find nothing there, she clicked on the link and was stunned to find a listing for her father at the very top of the page. The entry was followed by a nearly complete genealogy of the entire family, dating back several generations. What she'd been trying to compile on her own was there—in its entirety—right before her eyes! That "whoosh" that Natalie experienced had most certainly been her father's spirit, acting as a helper guide to assist her in answering her questions about her family.

The purpose of helper guides is exactly what it sounds like: to help make your life easier so that you can enjoy it. By serving you, they raise their own vibration, enjoy the afterlife a little more, and allow their own souls to grow. Very much like the ministry of angels (and often sent by them), helper guides assist you with specific tasks, special projects, or hobbies, and they come in several categories. Quite often, as was Natalie's case, they're deceased family members or friends who speak to you from the Other Side, offering their help because they love you.

Helpers are especially handy in areas where they had some level of expertise when they were alive. For example, I have a guide named Mr. Kay, who was my speech teacher when I was in grammar school, and who was one of my most beloved and understanding instructors. His spirit shows up whenever I make audio recordings, helping me avoid stuttering or making other mistakes, just as he did when I was in speech contests back in school. To my amazement, most of my audio work is nearly perfect the first time it's recorded—something I could never accomplish without Mr. Kay by my side.

Helper guides will very lovingly show up to lend a hand when you're stumped, blocked, or discouraged, which was very much the case when Dan, a recently widowed father of seven-year-old twin boys, came to me for a reading. Not only was he devastated by the loss of his wife to breast cancer, but he was frustrated because he didn't have anyone to care for his sons so that he could return to work. He'd tried two nanny agencies, but neither of them had provided him with the kind of care that could fill the void in his family's home . . . or their hearts.

By the time he showed up at my office, Dan was desperate. Luckily his helper guide came through, and from the message I got, I was sure that it was his wife. When he first asked, "What can I do?" all I heard in response were two words—*first communion.*

I asked Dan, "Are you Catholic?"

"No, I'm not," he said. "My wife was an Episcopalian who loved her church, and she went often with the boys—but I'm noncommittal when it comes to religion, so I only went occasionally."

"Do Episcopalians have first communion?" I asked.

"I think so," he answered. "Why? Do you think I should have the boys make their first communion? What does that have to do with finding the right person to care for the boys so that I can get back to work?"

"I don't know," I replied, "but your wife is suggesting just that."

"Well, that would be just like her," he said, as his eyes filled with tears. "I don't think it will help with my problem, but I'm willing to follow her wishes. . . . I just don't make the connection, though. Can you ask her to explain?"

When I relayed his questions, I got the same answer, so Dan accepted the message and went to his wife's church, where he enrolled his sons in first-communion classes. During the course of the boys' lessons, he met other parents and shared his story with them. A woman named Donna told him that her recently widowed mother was moving from Utah to live with her family the following week, and would soon be looking for a job. She assured Dan that her mother, who'd been a homemaker all her life, would be the perfect nanny.

A week after arriving from Utah, Donna's mother showed up at Dan's door, ready to work, love, and nurture all three of them. The connection was unbelievable, and five years later, she's still with them and has become the anchor of their family.

It's important to note that helpers don't necessarily have to *do* something to be helpful. I think in many ways that their greatest gift is letting us know that life goes on beyond death and that the spirit doesn't die—even when the body does. Losing the fear of death helps us live our lives to the fullest, which is perhaps the helpers' greatest mission. For instance, my husband's younger brother, Dennis, crossed over to the Other Side many years ago, yet he visits our home all the time. Dennis loved to ride bikes with Patrick when they were young men (they even bicycled across the U.S. once)—and he's still present when my husband rides today, especially out in the country. Patrick says that he feels his brother riding next to him, leading him to discover new trails and interesting nooks along the way.

Dennis also loved flowers, and I often feel him when I'm in our garden. In fact, every time I see a new flower outside, I feel his loving spirit alongside it. I cherish these times and know that Dennis is there to help me appreciate life.

Similarly, my mother communicates with *her* mother (my nana) all the time through her dream state. The two were separated during the war when Mom was a young child, so she's thrilled to have reconnected with Nana when she dreams. Sometimes they go to a beautiful place where they listen to gorgeous music, and they dance and sing together all night long; while other times, Nana gives her tips on sewing and making patterns—a creative passion they share. She even tells jokes, which my mother remembers and shares with us. And sometimes she's just *there,* giving Mom her love and company.

In addition to past family and friends, helpers can also be spirits who've had no relationship to you presently, but who *did* have strong connections with you in past lives. They often show up to continue to help you grow in areas you've worked in together in the past. For example, I have two beloved helper guides named Rose and Joseph who help me a great deal with my mission in life as a six-sensory teacher and a healer. I feel them with me as I encourage people to open their hearts and to love themselves and life more. I'm sure I knew these spirits in past lives, and our work together, even then, was to guide, counsel, and direct people in very much the same way that I do today.

I also work with The Pleaidean Sisters, guides who help me when I give readings—especially when I'm directing people to their soul path or higher purpose. According to these sisters, I've been their student for lifetimes. I know that they're essential to my work, and I rely on them greatly for direction with all of my clients.

Did You Know That
Helper Guides . . .

. . . were all human at one time, and their vibration and frequency is still very much connected to the human plane?

. . . usually communicate telepathically with you in words or short messages that you pick up in your mind?

. . . like to connect with you in your dream state, usually in some sort of friendly conversation?

. . . rarely elaborate on their input—which can be challenging if you're a control freak or think things to death—since their directions usually require instant acceptance if you hope to be helped?

. . . retain the knowledge and skills they learned while in human form and are committed to sharing them with you before they move on to higher frequencies?

. . . help you in order to bring closure to *their* earthly connection, so they can move on to higher vibrations and other soul experiences?

You may also attract helpers who come to you because they love what you're working on and want to share their knowledge and expertise with you. Their connection with you is more impersonal, since they're not connected with you from the past. In fact, they're often sent to you by the ministry of angels, who know that a particular helper can draw from their past lives to help you in an area where you may not know what to do.

These guides may be doctors who assist you with your physical health, or money managers or bankers who help you attract or better manage your money. They may even be odd-job workers or fix-it wizards who help you repair things—such as the mechanic guide I mentioned earlier who helped jump-start my car when it stopped running in traffic.

My father is a master handyman (among other things), and for as long as I can remember he's been able to fix anything that breaks down, including televisions, vacuums, refrigerators, DVD players, air conditioners, and even washing machines and dryers. Amazed at his skill, I once asked him where he learned to be so handy, to which he replied, "I didn't actually learn from anyone. I simply follow my inner guide who tells me what to do, and together we seem to figure it out." Dad must have quite a talented helper, since he always gets the job done.

Note that some of your helpers stay with you all your life, while others are more temporary and only step in for a short time to assist with a particular project or assignment. If you're willing to listen to their guidance, these guides will stick around and see things through to the end. If, on the other hand, you ask for aid and then perpetually ignore it, they'll step away. They're there to help, but they'll never force you to accept their assistance, so if you insist on doing everything your way and never consider their input, they'll respect you and pull back.

The key to working successfully with any of your helpers is to quiet your mind and trust what comes to it, rather than allowing skepticism or logic to shoot down their suggestions. You may hear their instruction in only one or two words (or a few more if you're lucky), and often they'll only repeat their direction once, so as not to interfere with your free will—it's up to you to pay attention so that you don't miss it.

Diane, a Realtor, was a student in a class I taught in upstate New York who shared a beautiful example of the benefits that unfold if you're willing to listen to your helpers without hesitation or resistance. It seems that one day she was on her way home from an open house when she got a call that a new house had just been put on the market. She decided to drive past it to see what it looked like, and when she arrived, she felt an instant attraction to the place. Suddenly a distinct voice said, *Buy it,* loud and clear.

Diane already owned two houses and was financially stretched to her limit, but her helper guide again insisted, *Buy it. . . .*That's all she heard, but it felt right, and that was enough for her.

"Okay, I will," she said aloud, adding, "but you need to help me."

When she went home and told her husband what had happened, he reacted negatively, asking, "What about your plan to buy a dream cottage near the ocean?"

Yet Diane didn't back down. She couldn't believe her resolve—she rarely trusted her gut so clearly (and she never stood up to her husband), but in this case, she was adamant in her decision to listen to her helper. She realized that she was tired of missing her moments of opportunity out of fear and hesitation, and was ready to give her intuition a chance. When she expressed her unwavering intention to listen to her guide, her husband backed down, which was something that had never happened before.

That night Diane told her son, Ryan, who was married and renting her second home, about her plan to buy the property. To her surprise, he asked, "Mom, would you mind if I bought the house rather than continue renting from you?"

Ryan had never indicated that he'd wanted to move—let alone buy a house of his own—yet the minute he said it, it resonated with Diane. Together they made an offer on his behalf, and three weeks later the house was theirs.

The best part of the story was yet to come: Since Ryan had moved out of her second home, Diane was now free to put it on the market. It sold for three times what she'd paid for it in a matter of weeks, and suddenly she had more than enough money to buy her dream cottage at the ocean—which she and her husband found shortly after. While this may all sound far-fetched, it's actually a classic example of the benefit of having helper guides: In less than two months, a whole stream of related desires were made possible because Diane accepted their help.

It's also important to pay attention to your dreams, as they're often the portal through which your helper guides connect with you. My client Patricia, for instance, felt that her helper was her deceased dad. Their relationship hadn't been very close when he was alive because he'd buried himself in his work as an investment banker, but this changed soon after his death. She began dreaming of him—always in the context of his offering her financial advice—which eventually evolved into a daytime connection, where she even heard his voice in her head.

An aspiring film producer, Patricia moved from Michigan to California, where her father continued to advise her—particularly when she was interviewing with a prospective employer at a production company where she really wanted to work. She was so flattered that she was even in the running for what she considered her dream job, and was so eager to get her foot in the door, that she would have accepted the position for free if they'd asked her to.

As Patricia and her interviewer discussed terms, she strongly felt her father's presence, and before she had a chance to respond to the woman's starting offer of $27,000, she heard her dad's voice say *$33,000.*

His input was so unexpected that she gasped, startling both herself and the interviewer, who, to Patricia's surprise, said, "Well, perhaps that *is* a little low . . . maybe we can go as high as $30,000 if you're willing to work the hours."

Again Patricia's dad piped up, *$33,000,* and his voice was so clear and forceful that she echoed it aloud: "$33,000."

"So that's your final offer?" asked her prospective employer. "In that case I'll have to discuss it with my partner. You have a very good résumé and apparently solid skills, but $33,000 is more than we were willing to invest in the position. I'll have to get back to you."

Patricia was sure that she'd lost the job, and as she got into her car, she told her dad, "I know I'm worth $33,000, but I wonder if *they* will."

Again, he simply said, *$33,000.* And an hour later, she got a call offering her the job on her terms.

I find it interesting that helpers often show up just to lend a hand or solve a problem, and then once it's addressed, they move on. A prime example of this occurred when Patrick and I bought our first home, which we had to renovate completely. Since this was something neither of us knew how to do (nor did we have the money for it), we worked on naiveté and pure panic. We began by tearing out everything so that we could start from scratch.

The one thing that bothered me more than anything else about the house was that the first-floor dining room was very dark and had no windows; however, if we *did* put a window in, it would have faced the ugly side of the building next door. Patrick suggested that we use lighting to brighten up the room instead, but I didn't take to that idea. I knew that there had to be a solution that wasn't expensive and was easy to execute, so one night I asked my helpers to give me some ideas before I went to sleep.

I dreamed that I was met by a tall, beautiful Roman man in sandals who walked me through church after church, pointing out all of the stained-glass windows for me to admire. Three or four times he mentioned how beautifully the sun shone through the glass, lighting up everything brilliantly.

I woke up feeling as if I'd been on vacation. As I recounted my dream to my husband, it dawned on me that my Roman helper was telling me to use stained glass in the dining room.

We could put in a lovely stained-glass window, get the light and color, and avoid the unpleasant view. It was a perfect solution, and one I never would have thought of myself. I loved the idea, and so did Patrick . . . but where to begin?

Again, thanks to my helper, even that was handled. The next day I read for a client, and afterward he asked me about the house. I shared our trials and tribulations with him, including the stained-glass idea. He said that he knew the best stained-glass artist in the area—and since the man had just arrived from Europe, he was willing to work for a modest price while he established himself.

To make a long story short, that afternoon my husband and I contacted the artist, and he was delighted to design us a stained-glass window at a price that was barely more than that of an ordinary window. Once installed, it was breathtaking and let in light and color, while completely blocking the ugly view.

A year later, not surprisingly, the artist's reputation grew and he began winning awards—he was even featured in an architectural magazine. Having one of his windows in our home raised its value considerably when we sold it.

As for my Roman helper . . . well, after that dream, I never saw him again.

Celebrities in the Spirit World

The most interesting helpers tend to be deceased famous people. And if you wish, you can actually invoke such past masters to help you. For example, I often call on the famous medium and spiritualist Edgar Cayce to help me with my work as a psychic, especially on issues of health and past lives. In many cases, he's helped me understand these issues better than any other guide.

My friend Julia Cameron, the well-known writer and playwright, invokes Rodgers and Hammerstein to help on her musicals; and John Newland, the famous director, to help her with her plays. Similarly, a client of mine who's a young female doctor regularly invokes research chemist Marie Curie to help her with proper diagnosis.

Celebrity helper guides are wonderful for aiding with creativity, as evidenced by my friend, rock star Billy Corgan. Billy once told me that, while working on his first solo album, *The Future Embrace,* he felt as though he were being fed specific musical compositions from masterful musicians in the heavens. And after hearing his music, I was sure that he was helped, as it carried a beautiful celestial energy.

I know of another young songwriter who invokes the spirit of John Lennon to help him write songs; and just look at all the people who have invoked Elvis Presley—obviously he's helping or there wouldn't be an entire industry of people perpetuating his great music, making a living at it, and having a blast doing so!

My mother began studying painting by taking correspondence classes when I was a young girl. She was so intent on becoming proficient at it that she progressed rapidly, and before long she started entering contests. Whenever she got stuck on a project, she sat down and prayed for help. In response, a Renaissance painter named Fra Angelico showed up in her dream state to give her specific tips on how to improve her work. He guided her through one particularly difficult painting, and did such a good job at instructing her that she won a national contest with it!

Invoking famous people to help you may seem like a bold or outrageous idea, but why not? These souls took their talents to a masterful level and are more than willing to share what they've learned from the Other Side. After all, Hillary Clinton invoked Eleanor Roosevelt to help her when she was First Lady. At the time, people laughed, but I thought it was brilliant. . . And considering all that occurred while Mrs. Clinton was in that position—and where she is today—I'd say that she was definitely helped.

Even my daughter, who's challenged by math and science, has no inhibitions about asking for the very best tutors to aid her, including Einstein (whom she calls on a regular basis). Does he answer? Well, she passes her classes—and even got A's this year—so I think he definitely does.

If you need assistance in a special area and can call to mind a famous person who's crossed over into spirit, simply identify them and invoke their support. To do this, get a picture of them if you can; if not, write down their name, meditate on their spirit, and then request that they come forward to help you. There's no need to beg since they're in spirit and don't have egos anymore—just ask for help, plain and simple, and be as specific as you can.

And here's a word to the wise: Sometimes people tend to act a little silly around famous people and make themselves small in their presence . . . even dead ones, believe it or not. Just remember that on a soul level, we're all part of one spirit and one family that simply resonates at different levels—but there's no separation. So when asking, remember that their role is to support your creativity and not to simply give you their ideas. Helpers (even famous ones) don't see you as small: You're magnificent, and they know this and want to help you discover it, too.

Your Turn

To invoke your helper guides—famous or familiar, friends or family, personally known or otherwise—focus on which areas you'd like help in and then ask for the highest level of expertise to assist you. It's wonderful to call in past family members or friends, but be careful—just because they're out of body doesn't necessarily make them instantly enlightened.

If they were talented in a certain area when they were alive, your loved ones can be helpful from the spirit plane in that area as well. But if your mother was a hopeless gambler, for example, don't seek her help on debt. By contrast, if your grandmother was happily married to the same man for 60 years before she died, she might be a great resource to help you with your marriage difficulties or relationship challenges. Just remember to use common sense when asking for help, just as you would when asking people for help on this plane. Open your heart, quiet your mind, and listen for their guidance . . . it *will* come.

Chapter 15

Healer Guides

One of the most beautiful groups of guides you'll ever connect with is your healers, who come in two forms: (1) those who have been healers, doctors, or caretakers in past human incarnations and focus on healing your body; and (2) those who come from very high energetic frequencies but may never have been in human form, who heal your spirit.

As a rule, they use every means possible to attract your attention, including communicating telepathically, appearing in your dreams, nudging you physically, and causing other sensations in your body. They may also send agents to bring you messages and have been known to go to great lengths to direct you to the right place at the right time. They'll use any clever maneuver they can.

These beings are subtle at first, but they turn up the volume and intensify their efforts according to the severity of your situation, doing everything in their power to get through to you. And unlike your helper guides, you don't have to ask for their input—they've made a soul commitment to guide you throughout your life.

Members of this group don't interfere with your choices, but they do let you know when the choices you make aren't in alignment with your health and well-being. For example, my client Tom was recently diagnosed with type 2 diabetes. He said that for more than 15 years, every time he reached for a second piece of cake or a third bottle of beer, he'd feel a slight physical tension and a small voice in his left ear saying, "Too much, too much."

He dismissed it as just being his conscience nagging him, but deep down he sensed that it was something more. The voice and tension felt as though they weren't coming from inside, but rather from someone next to him. And because he was slender and didn't indulge all that much, no one else ever suggested that he cut back.

When he received the diagnosis, he asked, "How did this happen?"

His doctor replied, "Who knows? It could be genetics, or maybe bad habits. Or it might be too much of the wrong things in your diet—amounts that are okay for others, but not for you." Hearing "Too much" was no surprise to Tom, because his healer guides had been telling him that for years.

These spirits not only warn you when personal choices could cause harm, but they also alert you to environmental problems. They once brought my husband a life-saving message while we were living in our first home, a redbrick two-unit flat on the north side of Chicago. We were both self-employed and had set up offices in our home that fall, with mine on the first floor and his in the basement.

Patrick worked downstairs for hours at a time, but one day he simply couldn't sit still at his desk. All day, he kept getting a message to go into the furnace room. He acted on it each time, and although he never found anything out of order, it continued to bother him.

Just before we went to bed, he recounted these events and said, "I don't know what's going on, but I'm going to call the repair people tomorrow to take a look and make sure that everything's okay before the weather turns really cold."

The next day a furnace expert arrived at noon and discovered a very slow carbon-monoxide leak. He told us that it was too small to be dangerous with the doors and windows open, but it was a good thing we'd found it now—because once we closed up the house for the winter, it could have killed us. Thank God the healer guides got through to Patrick that day!

Spiritual Referrals

These spirit assistants also work indirectly by placing you in the presence of people who'll give you information that you need to stay healthy, such as a new screening test or treatment, or even something as simple as the right doctor. The events often seem accidental, but they aren't; there's clever orchestration involved to put you at the right place at the right time to get what you need.

For example, one day I made an appointment to have a facial—which I seldom do—but rather than going to the neighborhood salon, I was guided to drive two suburbs away to see a woman who worked out of her home. I'd known her for years as a client, but had never considered using her services before my healer guides said, *Go to Erica,* in my mind just as clearly as if someone had spoken to me out loud.

"Erica?" I asked. "Isn't she a bit far away for just a facial?"

Go to Erica, I heard again . . . and so I went.

She was delighted to see me and couldn't have done a more conscientious, loving, and professional job on my skin. As she worked, I told her about the constant battle my younger daughter, Sabrina, was having with migraine headaches, severe bellyaches, and sleepless nights—the cause of which none of her doctors could pinpoint. This had been going on for years and had made her life miserable.

"I know who to see," Erica said and told me about a noted nutritionist who might be able to help. This approach had never occurred to me, and I felt tremendous relief that I could now do something to aid my daughter.

Taking this tip as a message from the healers—and the real reason I was sent to Erica—Sabrina and I went to the nutritionist, who determined that my daughter was allergic to wheat and dairy products and cut both of them from her diet right away. Although she didn't experience the instant miracle cure that I was hoping she would, the change eliminated 95 percent of her problems within a month, including many trips to the emergency room.

As they showed with my daughter, these guides are often useful in assisting with ailments that confuse medical doctors, and they try to help our earthly healers as much as possible. This was the case for my client Louise, who at age 36 was the picture of health, and, in fact, a fitness fanatic. An avid runner, very conscientious about her diet, and devoted to other such behaviors, she couldn't understand why her health began to deteriorate. To her horror, in the course of one year she went from being a vibrant young woman to a nearly incapacitated invalid for no apparent reason. Her energy dwindled, leaving her almost totally bedridden; her hair fell out, her vision blurred, and her mind wouldn't focus.

Diagnosed variously as with depression, Epstein-Barr virus, chronic fatigue syndrome, lupus, and even bipolar disorder, she had test after test, but nothing conclusive was discovered and her condition worsened.

In the meantime, she lost her job, her partner in life, and her will to keep going. In desperation, she came to me for a reading, hoping that I could help.

"Am I losing my mind?" she cried as she sat down in my office. "I can hardly get up to go to the bathroom, and the doctors tell me that I'm just depressed. Will this ever go away?"

I asked both my healers and hers what the problem was. They were very clear and direct: "Diet," they answered.

"Diet?" she scoffed. "How can that be? I eat nothing but vegetables and fish. I have a great diet, better than most."

"The guides say 'diet,'" I insisted.

"But I eat no meat or sugar or processed food, so how can that be the problem?"

"Maybe it's the fish," I answered

"How can it be the fish? Fish is good for you."

"I don't know," I said. "Ask your doctor about it. Maybe he knows something that we don't."

Louise started to leave. She was disappointed that neither my guides nor hers could get a better read on her illness, and she let me know it.

I was let down, too. I'd hoped to give her something more helpful from the guides, but I never have control over what they say. Still, their message was so clear that I felt it would eventually make sense.

"I'm sorry you're disappointed," I said at the door, "but don't rule out what came through. Just ask your doctor next time and see what he says."

A week later, Louise called back: "Sonia," she said, "guess what? The doctors finally think they know what's making me so sick, and you told me first! It's mercury poisoning from all the fish I've been eating. Thank you very much."

"Don't thank me," I said. "Thank your healer guides. They're the ones who pointed out the problem."

Assistance in situations such as Louise's is wonderful, but these spirits work on more than just physical health. They also diligently attend to your soul, which can get sick and fragmented due to depression, drugs, alcoholism, trauma, and abuse, especially in childhood. They work on your energy field as well, which can become depleted due to a weak identity, low self-esteem, exhaustion, or poor personal boundaries.

They did just this for my client Noah, who suffered for years from depression and substance abuse. His struggle took a colossal toll on his life: His wife left him, he went bankrupt, and his kids stopped talking to him. It wasn't that he wasn't trying to sober up and, in his words, "grow up." He tried medication for depression, 12-step programs, and even went to group therapy. In his heart, however, he felt more comfortable blaming everyone else for his choices than getting real with himself—that is, until his drinking buddy and fellow self-pity addict suddenly died from a brain aneurysm.

Devastated, he saw the emptiness of his wasted self-destructive years and went to bed crying. And for probably the first time in his life, he asked for help from "someone out there" and meant it.

Noah fell into a deep slumber in which he entered what some call a "lucid dream." He found himself standing next to a very tall, beautiful, bearded man in a long red and gray coat with black boots. They both looked down at Noah's sleeping body.

My client said to the dream man, "I'm sick of myself. Is there any cure for that?"

The man gave him a profoundly heart-penetrating smile and said, "Forgive your past, be of service, cleanse your body and mind of toxins, and serve God . . . and know that we are here to help you."

Noah woke up still hearing the man's voice in his head, and for the first time in his life, he felt as if someone cared about him and could help. With that, his crazy lifestyle was over, and he ended his self-destructive behavior. Some very deep wound within him had healed.

He called it a miracle, and I do, too. At the age of 46, he went back to school to become a teacher, something he'd deeply desired but never had the courage to do.

I've witnessed many miracles through the grace of God and the assistance of beautiful healer guides. The most important part of their work is to teach you to have faith so that you can step out of your own way and allow the Universal Divine forces of heaven to come through you to heal your body, mind, and soul.

Hands-On Healing

Last fall, my friend Lilly, who'd recently moved from Bulgaria to Chicago, suffered a cracked tooth and found herself suddenly in great pain and distress. Needing a dentist fast—and one who could speak Bulgarian at that—her options for immediate help were limited to a female practitioner who had a less-than-stellar reputation. Not willing to withstand the agony of searching for a better option, Lilly decided to go ahead and work with this person, but before she sat down in the chair, she began fervently praying to her healer guides to come to her assistance.

Closing her eyes as she opened her mouth, she suddenly saw in her mind's eye a tall, fiery-looking shaman with red flames for hair, who announced himself as Zonu. Reassured by his presence, Lilly asked him to guide the dentist to do a good job in repairing (and hopefully saving) her tooth. Seconds later, another guide appeared, a woman named Madame Q, and conferred with Zonu.

The next thing she knew, these two were working together, guiding the dentist's hand as they took over the procedure. Only 20 minutes later, the dentist—to her own astonishment—announced that she was finished. In that short time, she'd managed to not only save the tooth but also rebuild it to perfection, something she'd never succeeded in doing before.

Not surprised, Lilly knew that this success was due to Zonu and Madame Q's help. She thanked the dentist profusely and said, "I had no doubt that you'd be able to do a perfect job for me."

Flattered, and a little confused by how quickly and successfully this procedure had taken place, the dentist confessed, "Truthfully, I don't know quite how it happened. I'm embarrassed to say that I wasn't even concentrating as I should have been, but was thinking the entire time of painting my house. The next thing I knew, I'd finished the repair, and I must say that it's the best work I've ever done in my life."

Lilly laughed and then replied, "It's not important how it happened. The point is that you did a great job, and now I can go home happy—so thank you." But in her heart, Lilly was really thanking Zonu and Madame Q, for she knew that it was their mastery that had brought about such perfect and rapid success. What impressed her most was how the guides were able to borrow someone else's hands to do their work while the woman daydreamed. With their assistance, Lilly experienced nothing short of a miracle in the world of dentistry—a saved tooth and a low bill!

The highest purpose of your healer guides is to restore your self-awareness and self-esteem as children of God and help you accept the love and unlimited blessings that God grants you. Opening your heart and mind to your worthiness is the best healing of all.

This is evident in my client Julie's experience. This 37-year-old woman had just emerged from an acrimonious five-year divorce battle in which she lost her home and the custody of her two sons. No sooner had the ink dried on the divorce decree when she was dealt another devastating blow: Discovering a lump in her right breast, she was diagnosed with stage-4 breast cancer and given a bleak prognosis, with little chance for survival. Still reeling from the toll of her familial troubles, this was almost too much to bear. Pulling herself together, she immediately began aggressive treatment, including a double mastectomy, radiation, and chemotherapy—but not only did her treatment leave her broken and sick, it wiped out her will to live as well.

One night as Julie lay drained from nausea and grief, she decided that it wasn't worth trying to live, and she gave up. She'd lost her body as she knew it, her boys, her home—even her identity as a wife and mother—and felt that there was nothing left. Despairing, all she wanted to do was die.

When she eventually fell asleep, she dreamed that she was surrounded by ten beautiful women of all ages, who were gently singing lullabies, combing her hair, and rubbing her feet and toes as if she were the most precious child on Earth. Starting to cry, she asked why they were being so good to her.

The eldest one smiled and said that they'd come to help her heal and begin to enjoy her life. Julie responded that she had nothing to live for and that she was a complete failure, but the woman simply smiled again and kept combing her hair and singing with the rest.

Allowing herself to enjoy their loving care, Julie began to relax on a profound level—deeper, in fact, than she'd ever felt in her life . . . and the next thing she knew, it was morning. It seemed as if all that remained of the dream was a warm sensation in her chest, yet there was something else.

Remarkably, she felt peaceful and wanted very much to live. It was as if those women had lifted the weight of her grief.

Not looking back or feeling ashamed anymore, Julie dove into her healing with a vengeance. She changed her diet, joined a support group, and got a therapist and a coach. Two years later, she was proclaimed cancer free, and that was seven years ago. "Those women worked a miracle on me," she told me.

"They were your healers," I answered, "and they did. They opened the door for you to love yourself, and *that* is what healed your body."

Did You Know That Healer Guides . . .

. . . will always leave you feeling peaceful, self-loving, and self-accepting?

. . . are gentle, noncoercive, and forgiving?

. . . speak to your heart, not your ego—to your eternal essence, not your mortal self?

If you suffer from a lack of faith, it means that somewhere along the way you got disconnected from your loving Divine

Source and Creator. Like a beautiful flower without a garden to grow in, life without faith becomes a struggle to survive. This is perhaps the greatest drain on your health—body, mind, and soul—and something that you should ask your healer guides to restore.

They'll respond by opening your heart, quieting your mind, and raising your vibration. My healer guide Joseph once said to me that his work is a lot like rebooting a computer and clearing it of all the old useless programs and viruses; he removes the negative patterns so that balance is restored.

Your healers can do remarkable things for you, but only if you follow their direction and cooperate by loving yourself. Start by knowing that in each illness lies a great opportunity to learn, love, and honor yourself, and to accept God's love. And when this Divine affection isn't blocked, then healing can occur.

Please understand that I'm not saying because you have an illness or a deep life struggle that you've somehow failed. Each soul takes on challenges for reasons that no one else can judge or fully understand. What that's combined with environmental toxins, emotional stresses, and karmic soul lessons in which you must face the consequences and repercussions of poor choices in the past, this life, or beyond, it's virtually impossible to determine a simple reason behind any imbalance. All illnesses are lessons, either for the person who experiences them or for those around that individual.

The first lesson the healer guides share is: "When it comes to illness (or life for that matter), don't judge—not yourself, not anyone, not ever!" And the second lesson is: "Forgive— first yourself, then everyone else." If you're willing to take these two steps, you'll clear the way for these beings to do their work.

It's important to note that your healing guides aren't a substitute for seeking professional medical, psychological, and emotional care when you need it. In fact, another one of their important jobs is to steer you to find the right professional help.

They did this for me after the birth of my second daughter, when my body collapsed into deep chronic fatigue; no matter how much I slept, I kept feeling worse. I went to endless doctors and underwent endless tests, to no avail.

I asked my healer guides for help, and then the next day I went to Barnes & Noble to pick up some items for my elder daughter. While I was there, a book on hypothyroidism fell off a shelf—and almost onto my head. Needless to say, it got my attention, even though I'd been tested for the disorder before. My doctor at the time said that my thyroid-hormone level was borderline and not a problem, but after reading the book, I knew that something wasn't right.

My healers then made me aware of a holistic doctor, whom I visited for a second opinion. My levels were still marginally okay, but he put me on a very low dosage of natural thyroid anyway, and that did the trick. One month later, my energy level rose and I had my life back. Once again, the healer guides both pointed out the problem and led me to the right doctor for treatment.

My experience with the book isn't unusual, since that's one of the major means through which these guides communicate. My teacher Charlie told me that if a book is recommended to you once, it might be a sign from the healers; if people mention it to you twice, then it's definitely a message from them. And if you hear about it three times, they're screaming at you to pay attention!

These spirits are overseen by the healing angels and work on a very high frequency, with the greatest degree of love and compassion. Similar to your helpers, many of these guides have also been in human form at some point, so they understand the particular challenges of the human experience and what causes people to become sick and imbalanced. Many of them are from the lost civilizations of Atlantis and Lemuria, and have come to share the knowledge that they acquired but wasted or misused in their past incarnations. All the ones I've worked with have been tireless, devoted, and felt very privileged to help.

As is the case with all guides, however, they can't *make* you well and balanced; you must do that for yourself. They work under the motto "God helps those who help themselves," but they are your partners in health—and if you follow, they'll lead the way.

Your Turn

To invoke your healers to open your heart or mend your body, you must first find compassion and love for yourself and be willing to be healed. With your cooperation, they'll know exactly what to do.

To invoke healers on another's behalf, open your heart to theirs and send the same unconditional love and compassion to them. Don't focus on the illness, since to do so would be like watering a weed to make it grow. Instead, focus on 100 percent wellness according to God's plan.

In both cases, the next step is prayer, to which healer guides respond immediately. Myriad studies have confirmed that those who pray and are prayed for heal more fully and quickly than those without this aid.

My favorite healing prayer is:

Divine Mother God, Father God, and all healing forces of the Universe,
restore me to balance in body, mind, and spirit.
Remove everything from my consciousness and body
that isn't in perfect alignment with your loving plan for me.
I give my full permission and cooperation to all healing forces of Divine and loving nature to serve my well-being.
Amen

Chapter 16

Teacher Guides

Some of our soul's most devoted guides are our teachers. They resonate at a very high frequency and work closely with us to raise our awareness and understanding of our true nature as spiritual beings, concentrating their efforts on helping us discover our purpose in life as well as our karma, or lessons. In fact, the word *karma* means "to learn" and implies a sense of a classroom.

Unlike runners and helpers, these spirits have little or no interest in the day-to-day affairs of our lives. They don't concern themselves with questions such as "Will I get married?" or "Should I buy a new car?" Instead, their attention is directed to freeing you from the limitations of your ego and expanding your awareness so that you can fully embrace your unlimited potential to live in joy as a Divine being. They're also committed to guiding you in how best to serve your fellow humans. They help open your heart and dispel illusions, fear, judgments, false ideas, and self-imposed limitations.

Often, the same teacher guides oversee your soul's journey from one lifetime to the next. They group together to make up your soul's school, with each period you spend on Earth representing another level of advancement—much like being promoted to the next grade in school here on the physical plane.

Some of these beings have lived past lives as mortals, and as such, are sympathetic to the difficulties that humans face as they learn how to advance in life. They've often been wise men and women, mentors, or holy ones, and choose to continue this work on the spirit plane. They have great patience and compassion—and often much humor—as they strive to help keep you aligned with your soul's desires.

Although these guides may have taught you in past lives, they still must wait for a signal from you before they step forward and begin working with you again. Some of them may even have been instructors you've had in *this* lifetime, but who've crossed over in the recent past. I've spoken with many psychics, mediums, and other spiritual messengers over the years, and nearly all of them have at least one influential teacher who's passed over but who remains a strong guide in their soul's work. These continuing relationships are soul contracts that run deep and long and are not interrupted by death.

Two of my lifetime teachers, Charlie Goodman and Dr. Tully, both passed into spirit form many years ago, yet they continue to work closely with me from that plane. I feel their guidance as clearly as when I sat as a shy, young student in their respective classrooms years ago.

Charlie, my first teacher, taught me almost everything I know about the spirit world and was the first to introduce me to the proper protocol in working with many of my guides. I'm very aware of his presence when I help others learn—and even now, as I write this book. His particular calling card was (and still is) a laugh like a tumbling waterfall, with energy to match. His chortles remind me over and over that on a soul level all is well at all times, and that I should never get too worked up about anything.

I loved Charlie, and I'm grateful that I've been able to stay connected to him after his death. He knows my strengths and weaknesses, and every time I veer off my path because of insecurity, fear, judgment, impatience, self-righteousness, or anger, I hear his laugh shattering the spell I've fallen under. With it, I know he's bringing me back to center.

Dr. Tully, my other teacher from my past, was much less personal, but had no less of an impact on my learning process. He demonstrated again and again the direct correlation between my thoughts and my experiences. His detached style was part of his power, and through him I learned to be less emotional and more objective in my response to the world, a difficult lesson that I was grateful to learn (and with which I still need help). His powerful voice is his calling card; it cuts through my mental chatter and silences it immediately.

He taught me to tame my mind rather than entertain its confusion. He's also the one who showed me that my soul's purpose on Earth is to be creative—and to accept full responsibility for the life I create. To this day, whenever I slip into my childish victim mode, Dr. Tully's voice booms into my head reminding me of what Shakespeare said: "There is nothing either good or bad but thinking makes it so," . . . so watch your thoughts!

My most impressive teacher guides are known as the Three Bishops. They've been with me for several lifetimes, and I studied with them when I was a French priest examining ancient mysteries in the Middle Ages. The Three Bishops guide me and my clients in matters of decision making, and they focus on developing integrity and character. They're quite direct when pointing out poor choices and where mistakes were made. Although they don't mince words, their delivery is extremely loving and often humorous as they speak to the highest potential, in both me and my clients.

Perhaps you can think of someone who serves as your teacher in spirit. In fact, some of these guides can still be alive, and not only direct you in waking consciousness, but also visit you in your dreams or connect with you while you're in reverie. Much of our contact with teacher guides occurs at this time, as we're all too often preoccupied with day-to-day dramas in our waking lives to remember our higher callings. They also visit us during meditation, which is a wonderful way to have direct contact while in a conscious state. Their assistance will most likely continue after their death.

In my role and mission as a spiritual teacher, I've had hundreds of students report that I've come to them in their dreams or popped into their awareness out of nowhere. Some even see me in spirit as they struggle with issues, and I believe them. Spirit isn't defined by the physical body, so I can be in two places at the same time.

I must admit that at times when I awake, I feel as though I've been working all night helping and teaching my students, and their reports confirm it. Perhaps you've had this experience—on a soul level you're serving as a teacher to someone, and you, too, function in the spirit world while your body sleeps.

Two of my greatest teacher guides who are still on this plane are my mentors Lu Ann Glatzmaier and Joan Smith, two profoundly wise souls I've known since I was 14 years old. Not only do I connect with them on a waking level, but I also see them in my dreams. When I'm sleeping, I visit them regularly and have long, deep, soul-healing conversations, which I value as much as my phone and in-person connections. In this case, I'm the student visiting my teachers at night, sometimes having classes till dawn. I wake up exhausted when this happens, and perhaps a similar situation may be why *you* may awaken fatigued after dreaming about learning or instructing others.

It may surprise you to think of some of your teacher guides as living, or even to view yourself as a potential teacher guide, but we all have an ancient soul history, and we're strong—even masterful—in some areas, while we still have a long way to go in others. Both Charlie and Dr. Tully taught me that we're all both instructors and students of one another at the same time, because we're all connected like cells in a body—all showing each other how to grow on different levels.

You can also connect to ancient wise ones who acquired the spiritual awareness and discipline to quiet the mind and make direct contact with the Divine. They're very gentle, loving, and extremely patient beings who show up when you begin to question the nature and purpose of your life and want to live in a more meaningful way. Having worked hard for so long to dissolve their egos, many choose to remain anonymous.

These guides often direct you to certain lectures, workshops, seminars, and spiritual gatherings. Many of them focus on shifting the mass consciousness to a higher frequency and have been doing so since the 1950s with great success. The relatively low number of "hippies" in the 1960s has now expanded to thousands of people interested in spiritual topics, thanks in large part to these guides, who've brought meditation, relaxation, massage therapy, and intuitive exploration to a wider audience. They're also responsible, along with healer guides, for bridging the gap between science and religion, mainstreaming spirituality, creating fellowships such as 12-step programs and group therapy, and opening the door to alternative and holistic healing—all of which are pathways to greater learning on a soul level.

Did You Know That
Teacher Guides . . .

. . . are coming to us en masse now in virtually every area of learning and expertise? Through quantum physics, for example, they're teaching us that we are pure energy, pure spirit, and unlimited by anything other than our own thoughts. In virtually every discipline, they're ushering in new discoveries and wiping away old prejudices.

. . . reach out to us as our world is being seriously challenged—especially in our spiritual understanding of things?

. . . serve their main purpose in helping you shed any false identity that you may have connecting you to your ego?

. . . lead you to live fully and truthfully in your spirit?

One way in which teacher guides often work is by sending messengers who invite you to learning forums. Once, when I became overwhelmed by my marriage, kids, and work, I asked my teacher guides to direct me to what I needed to learn so that my life would flow easier. The very next day I was invited to the Hoffman Quadrinity Process, an eight-day intensive program where I could learn creative new strategies for living in my spirit. It turned out to be one of the best classes I've ever taken. (Check it out at **www.hoffmaninstitute.org**.)

Similarly, you'll know that your teacher guides are with you when you're no longer content with how you handle your life and want to learn more. For example, at the age of 40, Max was the picture of success on the outside: a handsome, single airline pilot with looks, money, and glamour. He was also the only son of a doting—but in his mind, demanding—old-school Italian mother. On the inside, however, he felt miserable, conflicted, and bored and saw his life as meaningless, resulting in a low-grade depression.

One day, sitting alone in an empty airplane in Cleveland as he waited for the crew and passengers to board, he closed his eyes to relax. Suddenly, he felt as though a higher presence had come to visit. It seemed to open a door in his mind that had been nailed shut. It was as if a benevolent force had freed his eyes and his heart, and he instantly realized that his life lacked satisfaction because he was so selfish and self-centered.

He heard no voice, and he saw no ghost from Christmases past. He just felt an inner opening that used to be blocked . . . and he saw where he was headed given the decisions that he was making. His negative behavior suddenly loomed large, and he felt ashamed and sad.

He was so appalled at what he'd become that he had trouble concentrating on flying that day. Fortunately, he made it to Chicago (where he was based) but was unable to meet his flight schedule. He called in sick because that's how he felt.

What followed was his dark night of the soul. With his teacher guides ever present, his new awareness kept expanding back through his life to the day that his dad had died, when Max was only 11—the day that his heart had slammed shut and he'd decided to think only of himself rather than go through the pain of loss again.

Realizing all this, he cried out, "What shall I do?" but he heard nothing. The next morning, still off from work, he went for a drive in the city and ended up at Transitions Bookplace, a tiny, hole-in-the-wall (at the time) New Age and self-help bookstore. Until he walked in and looked around, he'd never known there were such things as self-help books; to him, the word *spirit* meant only cocktails. He was fascinated, and spent three hours browsing. Then he bought ten books, some on the soul, some on purpose and direction, and some on meditation.

Max's spiritual journey began the day his guides led him to the mirror to see what he'd become. He was then directed to resources for a more authentic existence, first through the bookstore and from there to classes, workshops, and intuitive sessions with mentors and other instructors . . . and eventually to me.

His soul's growth was slow but steady: His teachers brought him to a group of volunteers who helped kids in developing countries who were in dire need of medical care. Time after time, Max flew them to the U.S. for treatment. It was so fulfilling that he cut his job to part-time and put most of his energy into this service. By helping these needy children, he opened his heart and learned to love again, fully and without defenses. His guides taught him well.

He'd realized their greatest purpose: to teach us to open our hearts and see the world and ourselves with love, to recognize that we're all one family with many colors. If we injure others, we hurt ourselves; if we aid others, we help ourselves.

Learning from the Masters

In addition to receiving soul instruction from our present and past teacher guides, we also connect to one, or at most two, master spiritual leaders. This group is known collectively as the Ascended Masters or the Brotherhood of the White Light, and they work with us both personally and impersonally to raise our consciousness. The most well known have walked the earth, such as Jesus, Mother Mary, Qwan Yin, Buddha, Mohammed, Wakantonka, and St. Germaine, to name a few.

Many people, including me, are deeply drawn to one of the first two as their master teacher. I have a client who's so connected to Mother Mary that she prays a rosary to her three times a day. This woman is the most loving soul I've ever met, having been a foster parent to more than 14 children over the years, and adopting 8 more. She believes that it's Mary—the mother of us all—who gives her the endless energy, patience, and faith to pursue this path so joyfully.

Maurice, another client, talks to Jesus nonstop about everything in his life, and I understand his devotion. Having lived through a house fire in which he lost his family and was burned over 40 percent of his body, he said that Jesus taught him to for give and get on with his life. He now tutors disabled and handicapped children and is at peace.

School's in Session

You know that you've entered the classroom of a teacher guide if your heart softens and you become quieter, more inclined to listen than talk. You're under their influence if you desire to read more on spiritual matters, become called to a fellowship or community intended to help you grow, or seek spiritual instruction in some direct way. You're especially following a teacher guide if you feel called to serve humanity in a deep, selfless manner.

The lessons are adapted to what's right for your soul. These beings know, as should you, that one size doesn't fit all when it comes to spiritual growth. One person's guides may send him to church, while those of another may take her away from church and direct her to a more personal relationship with God and the Universe.

Teacher guides especially want you to know that there's no one *right* way for you to be spiritually aligned with your soul. You must listen to your own heart, follow its guidance, be willing to be uniquely yourself, and run your life based on self-love and acceptance rather than fear or a desire to please others.

Don't ever worry about calling on your teacher guides too often. You're their number one priority through dark nights and confusion. When you ask, they'll step right in.

Your Turn

In a quiet space, gently ask your teacher guides to reveal themselves to you, first requesting that your Higher Self open your heart by taking a deep, relaxing breath. Then inquire, "What am I to learn right now, and how can you best help me to do so? What am I hiding from? What am I afraid of?"

Listen quietly, and if you're able to respond to this question out loud, let your heart speak as they guide you to the answer.

Your teachers, more than any other spirits, have impeccable standards for guidance. They don't isolate, praise, or flatter you, although they work hard to create a positive learning experience. They won't compare you to others. They'll only give suggestions, never ultimatums, but they *will* ask the most of you. They had you pick up this book, didn't they?

Teachers, like all guides, know exactly what you want. They'll take you step-by-step through a gentle learning curve and stay with you for as long as you need. Just remember, when the student is ready, the teachers appear. If you're ready, then so are they.

Chapter 17

Animal Guides

Some of the most important and powerful spirit guides are the most obvious, yet they're often overlooked: those of the animal kingdom. There was a time long past when we were closely connected to the natural world and consulted animals for their wisdom and personal power. But even though we've drifted away, this connection has never left us, and different creatures are continually communicating with us both in the physical world and in our dreams as they attempt to speak to our soul and spirit.

Animals are part of the teaching world. Some bring us the wisdom and skills to survive, while others show us how to morph and adapt, which can be very useful at times. They may be humorous and playful and teach us how to lighten up and laugh at life's challenges. Many are known for their loyalty and ability to love unconditionally; or perhaps they have a grounded detachment, remaining true to themselves rather than pleasing others. There are detectives and those with the capability to disappear. In one way or another, all of them have fantastic soul-awakening qualities and the ability to speak to us in their own manner.

Animals serve as spirit guides in three ways. First, they simply exist in our lives and communicate directly; second, they appear in our dreams, bringing messages through the astral plane. Third, by offering their spirits as totems, or gateways to access their particular power and energy, they help us accomplish our goals.

You can start connecting with your animal guides by seeing the spirit of the animals already present in your life. Begin with any pets you have (or have had), and focus on what their essence brings (or brought) you as a gift. My dog Miss T, a black miniature poodle, is a gorgeous, devoted, sensitive soul who works hard to love all my family members equally and unconditionally. One way she does this is by sleeping with each of us in shifts throughout the night. She starts in my room, then moves to my daughter Sabrina for a few hours, then on to my other daughter Sonia's bedroom until morning. She also sits with us one at a time: with me in my office when I do readings; at the foot of each of my daughters' desks when they do homework, sometimes pacing back and forth between them; and in my husband Patrick's office in the afternoons. When she's present, we all feel much calmer and happier.

We all recognize how psychic she is and how she communicates with us, no matter the time of day. When I'm awake, one look from Miss T will let me know if someone is or isn't okay. On the rare occasion that she growls or snarls at anyone, I know immediately that something about that person isn't right, and I should be on guard.

Once we hired a babysitter who came highly recommended and was very personable, but Miss T wasn't impressed. She barely tolerated the new addition and never took her eyes off her, letting us know that this person wasn't to be trusted. The sitter had worked for us for only a few days when we received a phone call from her frantic father, claiming that she was a runaway and that he wanted her home. We'd *felt* that something was amiss, but our little dog *knew* it, and we sent the girl home.

Miss T is a tremendously playful spirit as well, dancing for us, doing funny dog tricks, and playing catch and hide-and-seek when we're down. She's helped Patrick relax, stopped me from overworking, and kept my daughters from being scared and lonely. Her gifts are endless.

A few years ago, I'd felt that this sweet spirit wasn't herself, but thought that it wasn't anything too out of the ordinary. Then I dreamed she told me that she was sick and needed to see a doctor. So the next morning, I told Patrick to take her to the vet, but the doctor couldn't find anything wrong. Later that night, she sat at the foot of my daughter Sonia's bed and let her know that she needed help. Sonia pried her mouth open and found a small chicken bone lodged deep in her throat, which she removed. Miss T could have died, but the minute it was gone, she rebounded back to normal.

Cats are also incredible teachers and communicate with our souls. I've never owned a cat because I'm allergic to them, but my brother Anthony has had two tabbies, Summer and Winter

Girl, who've kept him grounded and amused through many emotionally challenging times of illness and stress. His cats' antics and calming presence have kept his heart open and happy when he could have easily shut down. In many ways, they were his healers, and he says so all the time.

Birds are another type of creature who will speak to you, and my client Marion has relied on them for guidance. He was about to undertake a new business venture that involved opening movie theaters with his brother-in-law, when he spotted an owl in his backyard two nights in a row. Knowing that these birds are predators who are active at night, he felt that it was a signal confirming his suspicion that his brother-in-law would be sneaky and aggressive. Thanking the owl for the warning, Marion declined to enter the partnership. Once he made that decision, the bird left.

Disappointed, his brother-in-law took on another collaborator. Eventually, he and the new partner began fighting over who owned what, and accounting cover-ups by both parties were revealed. The theaters closed, and lawsuits were filed. My client's personal relationship with his brother-in-law, however, remained intact—thanks to the owl.

Birds have also spoken to me in very direct ways over the years, affirming my path and guiding my spirit. Shortly after Patrick's parents had a terrible accident some years ago, black crows suddenly filled the trees in front of our house and began to caw, as if to bring us a message. I've always taken crows to signify power and magic, so I knew that their presence was important.

For ten minutes the crows called out at full volume, and then they flew away. I knew that they were telling us that my in-laws would be all right and not to be worried. I don't speak crow, of course, but in my heart and soul, I knew that's why they came. With their wisdom backing me up, I assured Patrick that his parents would fully recover, even though the outlook was bleak. They *did* get better, and to this day I thank the birds for letting me know at a time when it looked unlikely.

Another time, I was in a deep quandary over whether to write my autobiography, which I'd been asked to do. This happened when I was with my husband and children on vacation in France, visiting the host family I'd spent time with years earlier as a young student. Uncertain if my life story would be of any value to others, I asked my guides to give me a definite sign and then went to bed.

As if awakened by some higher force, I shot out of a deep sleep at five in the morning and looked out the window. Heading straight toward me was a beautiful white dove— which flew in through the bedroom window and hit me squarely in the head! Knowing from my teachers that birds are messengers of the soul, that startling sign assured me that writing the book was something I must do for my own soul, if not for others.

The poor dove got knocked for a loop and landed in a daze in the corner of the bedroom, but recovered her composure after a moment or two and flew out the window and into the sunrise. I wrote the book, and I don't know about others, but it was definitely good for *my* soul.

My nephew Jacob told me the following beautiful bird story. Feeling upset and missing his father on the first anniversary of his death, Jacob decided to go for a walk along a deserted Michigan beach near his home. As he walked, a magnificent bald eagle, the first he had ever seen in that state, seemed to come out of nowhere, and it soared above him. Jacob then looked down and saw a rose frozen in the ice. The events both shook him and strangely comforted him, and he knew that the eagle was a messenger.

This type of bird made an appearance on another occasion, when my dear friend Julia Cameron was agonizing over whether to move into a new apartment in New York that was closer to the central part of the city and far from where she'd been living on Riverside Drive. She feared that the change would remove her from nature's grass and trees, which she dearly loved. She decided to go through with it, however, and on the day of the move she saw a beautiful eagle sitting on the fire escape directly outside the window of the new apartment, welcoming her. Several other people saw it, too. It stayed there all day, as if to let her know that the apartment would serve her well, which proved to be true. She's done some of her best writing since arriving there.

If we pay attention to their lessons, animals teach us all the time. My sister Cuky, the eldest of seven siblings and the nurturer of all of us, was beginning a new career in healing. She was also a fraidy cat when it came to the natural kingdom, and she knew that it held her back. Although she loved her cats, she'd always avoided communing with nature and never even camped. Wanting to face her fears and become a profound soul healer, she took a trip to the Anasazi ruins in New Mexico with her best friend and shaman apprentice Debra Grace.

As they walked through the woods, animals appeared one at a time, peeking out from the foliage and spying on her.

One in particular, an enthusiastic red squirrel, saw Cuky coming and bolted directly toward her. It was running so fast that she was certain it was going to leap up and lunge at her before she could avoid it. Too afraid even to scream, my sister froze, whispering, "He's coming right at me. He's coming right at me."

Debra agreed: "Oh, my God, he is!"

Unsure of what to do, they both stood still as the squirrel raced toward them. Suddenly it stopped, inches from Cuky's face, and smiled at her. It stayed like that for a full ten seconds, then turned and ran away as fast as it had come. It was so funny and surprising that they both burst out laughing. The little creature was really too cute to be afraid of, and my sister realized that it had given her the gift of helping her overcome her fear of nature by literally looking her in the eyes.

A year later, Cuky went to Hawaii, lived off the land, and camped in a tent for an entire month while learning the ancient healing art of Lomi-Lomi from a native master, something she could never have done before the trip to New Mexico.

But animal guides aren't always cuddly. On a meditation retreat in the California mountains several years ago, Patrick decided to go for a walk. As he hiked, he became aware of just how much fear controlled his life. No sooner had he thought this than a vicious, menacing pit bull appeared out of nowhere, gnashing its teeth, snarling at Patrick, and preparing to attack. Having nothing with which to defend himself, and with his obvious terror tempting the animal like raw meat, Patrick suddenly remembered his meditation skills and quieted his fear through breathing and thoughts of peace.

The moment he relaxed (or at least attempted to), the dog stopped growling, turned away, and ran to its owner, who also appeared out of thin air. This growling beast helped my husband face his fear and choose to command it rather than let it control him. The moment he did, the dog retreated and Patrick returned safely to his room.

These are just a few examples of how closely animal guides can be connected to you and how they show up to teach you more about your spirit. Once you begin to notice these direct encounters, your mind will open up to the greater ways that these beings offer direction in your life—and they don't even have to be alive to do so!

Once I was riding my bike along the Chicago lakefront and nearly ran over a very large, smashed rat. Swerving to avoid it, I knew that this disturbing sign had a particular and timely message for me. Two thoughts came to mind: (1) Rats are less than savory, and (2) they live in my environment. Adding up the signs and evidence, I felt that the spirit of the dead rat was warning me of my undesirable community and the bad ending it could bring me if I didn't watch out. The more I thought about it, the more I had to acknowledge that there were several individuals I was connecting with at the time who didn't share my ethics and values and were in many ways quite ratlike. The rodent on the path was a message for me to step away from these people before something ended badly (as had happened to the animal), so I did.

A few months later, it came to my attention that one of these unsavory "rats" had stolen money and credit cards belonging to mutual friends and then left town to avoid prosecution.

It was indeed a bad ending, but due to the warning the dead rat in the road had offered me, I was spared the drama.

As that experience showed, all animals are teachers and bring healing messages, if we just pay attention. There are many other, more peaceful examples: Watching many fish in an aquarium, or even just one swimming in a fishbowl, brings a profound sense of well-being as they smoothly glide through the water. Turtles offer a sense of grounded protection as they teach you how to withdraw from the world and retreat into your own being whenever you feel stressed and overwhelmed. Hamsters teach you how to cooperate and have fun as you watch them play on their wheels and sleep together in their cages.

Did You Know That Animal Guides . . .

. . . are some of your most powerful spirit guides?

. . . endow you with qualities to enhance your life and activate your creativity and intuition?

. . . help return lost pieces of your soul and reconnect you to the natural world?

When connecting to your animal guides, notice how different creatures communicate in your dreams, because when they show up, their spirits are conveying something important to you, and are often coming to you as a totem to give you energy that you need. My client Tom had a vivid dream in which he was riding a beautiful, white stallion all night long, and he awoke invigorated like never before. It left such a strong impact on him that he knew that the animal had visited him for a reason.

Contemplating the experience, he remembered how powerful he felt during it—something he didn't feel when awake. The horse spirit came to give him power. Accepting the gift, he mustered the energy and will to quit his dead-end job, bring to a close a relationship that was going nowhere, and move to California as he'd long wanted to. After his dream, he sailed through these difficult decisions and got on with his life.

If your life is stagnant or in need of healing, you can actually request animal spirits to come and help you change your vibration and arouse your energy. Just remember that when calling these guides forward, it's the animal spirit who chooses you, not the other way around.

This chapter is only an introduction to these amazing beings. There are many wonderful books available on how to work specifically with animal guides, if you're interested in learning more. But for now, be open to all creatures—those in your life, those who cross your path, those in your dreams, and the animal guides who serve as your totem. They're to be loved, respected, and valued deeply for their help and service to your soul. If you allow it, they will serve you well.

Your Turn

Do you own a pet, or are you around other animals? Start connecting to these guides by appreciating the unique spirit in your own pet or any creature you engage with on a regular basis.

How would you describe their spirit? What lessons can you learn from them? What message or healing do you receive from them? Let your heart speak, not your head. Trust what you feel and don't censor your emotions.

Next, begin to recognize where animals show up in your life in other ways. For example, have you noticed any birds lately? How about deer or horses?

Think about whether there are any recurring animals presenting themselves to you in some way. Perhaps you keep meeting hawks, rabbits, or other wild beasts. Ask your spirit what these beings are trying to convey, and remember to trust what you feel.

To better harness the gifts of your animal guides, keep a journal by your bed and note any visitations by animals or birds in your dreams. At the minimum, tell someone (trustworthy, of course) about these experiences, because whenever a creature gets your attention, it's bringing you a spirit message.

If you want to take the initiative and get in touch with your totem animal spirit, you must use your imagination. Here's how:

1. Relax in a comfortable place where you won't be disturbed.

2. Imagine going into a cave or an old, hollow tree, and emerging in a natural setting such as a meadow or field.

3. Experience the peace and power of nature in this place.

4. Ask your animal guide to appear in this beautiful place and speak to you. Trust whatever animal appears and however it chooses to communicate. You may sense, feel, hear, see, or simply know in your heart that it's present.

5. Once you're connected to your guide, use your imagination and go back through the field or meadow to your cave or tree, and then step back into present reality. Take a moment to get grounded and slowly open your eyes.

6. Once you know what your animal guide is, study it to learn all that you can about it. There are many books on animal spirits, including those by Ted Andrews.

7. After you connect, thank your animal and ask it to send you a sign that it is indeed your spirit guide. The indication can appear in many ways: You may see its face on a card, in a picture, in a magazine, or on TV. You may even observe a live version. Be patient and it will appear. Ask for several signs of confirmation to be absolutely sure that it's your totem. Your guide doesn't mind and will send you more evidence.

8. Be aware of your animal spirit's presence in your life day by day, and use its particular energies to support and teach you. Pay attention to all expressions of its strengths, and be sure to thank your animal guide for helping you.

Chapter 18

Joy Guides

One of my most beloved groups are the joy guides. These are the child spirits of the Universe, and their job is to keep *your* inner child alive and well. Sometimes they're children who've lived and then crossed over when still very young, but more often, they've never been in human form. They have high, light, and joyful vibrations; they're very close to nature; and they work to keep us from taking ourselves and the human drama too seriously. They keep us from drowning in our misery.

Joy guides show up when they're least expected, usually when our egos are so drugged by our self-important suffering that we've lost all perspective and become isolated. This isn't to say that all our pain is self-imposed. There are times when we face true challenges and heartbreaking loss, at which point our angels and healers are in attendance to get us through.

Even then, however, these delightful spirits appear to distract us from our pain with their comedic antics, and when they do, we greatly appreciate their presence.

But they're more often inclined to appear when our egos have gotten the best of us and we're bent out of shape, such as when we work too much and refuse to have balance in our life. Joy guides are the enemies of workaholism and the antidote to this nasty addiction. Usually, when they appear and interrupt you, your response is irritation. Their favorite method is to send in your kids, who want to talk, play, and laugh. This sometimes works, but if you brush them off or don't have children, they use your pets to get you to take a break.

My friend Julia Cameron told me that when she's buried too deep in work and has become so absorbed that she's lost her sense of humor, her Highland terrier Charlotte drags over her ratty toy and insists on a game of fetch. My dog Miss T does the same for me. Our furry friends are regular emissaries of joy guides. Have you noticed how many self-important Hollywood types who are buried under the weight of their fame carry silly little dogs with them? Chihuahuas, Maltese pooches, you name it—they're on a mission from God to relieve these actors of the burden of their egos.

If you don't have pets, joy guides resort to other means to capture your attention. They may have the phone ring but with no one on the other line, or the doorbell rings and there's no one there.

It's especially fun for them to get us to laugh at the silliness of our egos. We're often annoyed at the assault—the dog's tricks, the baby's giggle, the child's happy nagging—on our self-importance. But the joy guides are relentless, and the more you resist, the more they tease. You can blow your top and try to send them and their adorable helpers scurrying for cover, but you'll feel like an ungrateful creep if you do. They're there to relieve you of your ego, not fight over it. If you simply give up the battle and laugh, you'll become balanced and escape the corner you've put yourself in.

In keeping with their mission, you never know when the joy guides will show up. Being spontaneous and silly pranksters, they especially love the element of surprise.

Just recently a client told me a funny story about these spirits. She and her husband had been suffering from their miserable marriage, each spending a great deal of energy trying to control the other and fighting most of the time. They agreed on nothing, continually argued, and spent the hours away from each other complaining about their spouse's outrageous behavior. One day it got so bad that they both said: "This has got to stop. We must divorce."

Finally agreeing on something, they very calmly (at least for them) began discussing how they intended to go their separate ways. As they were speaking, a fly flew in between them. While the husband spoke in a dead-serious tone about his need to be free, the insect landed on his nose. As he swiped wildly at it, his wife burst into laughter at how ridiculous he looked.

The situation was so absurd that he, too, had to crack a smile. And when he resumed his serious posture, the fly returned, landing right between his eyes. Refusing this time to acknowledge the fly's presence, he continued to rail while the bug strolled across his forehead. Again, his wife laughed uproariously, and in response, he slapped his head with such full force that she lost all control. He was doing to himself what she'd longed to!

Then it was her turn to air her grievances. As she started in on her laundry list of his transgressions, the fly landed on *her* face. She immediately went berserk trying to swat it away, only to have it dodge her as well. Her husband, of course, doubled over in glee. By that point, the silliness of it all was so infectious that she couldn't help but giggle as well. Their laughter escalated until tears rolled down their cheeks. They hadn't had that much fun together since they were dating.

Soon they were reminiscing about other shared moments of hilarity and spent several hours strolling down their memory lane of joyfulness. By the end, the husband said, "I'm sorry. I don't want a divorce—I just miss having fun with you." She felt the same way, so they called a truce and decided to give their marriage another try.

Will it work? I don't know. But with the joy guides present, at least they stand a chance.

Did You Know That
Joy Guides. . .

. . . bless your life so that your heart softens as your inner child is satisfied?

. . . help you begin acting like a loving adult—easygoing, generous, and more accepting of others?

Joy guides have only one purpose: to help us get over ourselves and remember how wonderful life is. They especially connect to babies and small children, entertaining them with crazy antics, which kids often mimic. If you've ever heard an infant in the nursery laughing and having fun all alone, you can be certain that the room is full of joy guides.

My daughter Sonia had a great connection to these beings as an infant, and with their help found all kinds of ways to entertain me. She was especially good at it when I was pregnant with my second daughter on the days when I felt frazzled and overwhelmed. At only seven or eight months old, she'd often see her joy guides and laugh out loud with them, knowing full well as she did this that she was making me laugh, too. There were dozens of times when I was fully prepared to sit down and have an indulgent feel-sorry-for-myself session, and she'd start to squeal and laugh and make such funny faces that I couldn't get down in the dumps. Through her, I felt the spirits dancing all around, and we'd both giggle so hard that everything I'd worried about faded away.

Laughter, especially the really silly, intoxicating kind, is the calling card of joy guides. If you ever want to find an abundance of them, go to places that attract children and pets. But remember that they don't just focus on kids and animals. As I mentioned, they also help lighten up overly serious adults, and show up to relieve extreme stress, especially in solemn gatherings where the pain and sorrow is often too much to bear. That's why you'll often find them at wakes and funerals.

I once attended a funeral for a friend's mother. She'd been a jovial, outspoken woman who insisted on having the last word on everything. Her sudden death from a heart attack left her family and friends heartbroken. In the middle of the priest's solemn eulogy, a cell phone rang, but no one dared to acknowledge it. The priest scanned the congregation to locate the culprit to no avail, so when the ringing finally stopped, the eulogy continued.

Moments later, another phone sounded from a different part of the congregation. Again, no one made a move to silence it. The priest, again interrupted and gravely displeased, waited until the ring subsided, then resumed speaking with a disapproving glare.

Then yet *another* ring tone echoed through the space. This time the priest lost all patience and said, "For Pete's sake, what is going on with all these cell phones?"

Little four-year-old Emily, one of the deceased woman's grandchildren, raised her hand and blurted out, "I know! I think it's Grandma calling from heaven to let you know you forgot to say how much she liked chocolate ice cream."

Everyone, including the dour priest, burst out laughing. Their grief was relieved and the eulogy switched from sorrowful words of loss to all the wonderfully funny moments that Grandma had brought to her loved ones. This was clearly a visitation by the joy guides, the practical jokers and comedians of the Universe.

As pranksters, one of their favorite antics is to hide things, often in full view. Have you ever missed your car keys on the way out the door, your passport just before boarding an international flight, or your tickets on the way to the theater? Frenzied, you eventually find them in a corner of your pocket, or even clutched in your hand. That's the work of a joy guide, telling you to take a breath, relax, and realize that everything will turn out well. They aren't malicious or nasty; they're just having fun with you to get you to lighten up.

They also love to hide jewelry, shoes, your wallet, purse, the report you've been working on, library books, your bathing suit, and your cell phone—anything to get you out of being on autopilot and bring you back into the moment. If you listen carefully, you can hear them giggling as they watch you race around like a chicken with its head cut off in those moments.

You can save yourself stress and time if you simply acknowledge the joy guides and go along with the joke. Just say, "Okay, I get it. I need to lighten up. Thanks for reminding me." If you do, the missing items will magically reappear.

Being eternal children, they like to play hide-and-seek with your runners. They hide things; your runners find them; just enjoy the game.

Besides keeping you from taking life too seriously, these spirits also connect you to what brings you happiness. They'll drag you into an art-supplies, toy, or music store; a dance or acting class; a drumming circle; or a travel agency for the trip you keep postponing.

They're the voice in your head that says it's okay to give yourself little treats, such as a Saturday to play with your kids— or to frolic as if you were a kid—to hang out with friends over coffee and conversation, to break out a board game with the family instead of all staring at the TV in silence. They remind you to go for that bike ride, take the beading class, and hang out and read a good book guilt free.

Start appreciating the joy guides around you. Open your eyes, ears, and heart to them. "Get over yourself," as my teacher Charlie used to say, "and get into your spirit" by paying attention not to what's wrong with this picture, as your ego tells you, but what's *right,* as your spirit reveals.

Feed your inner child with creative, joyful pleasures, and these guides will come dancing in. They love to help you do this by bringing you presents. My mom enjoyed giving these spirits assignments by asking them (and telling us to ask) for presents openly and often. On the way out the door to school in the morning, she'd remind us to ask for gifts—and expect them. "You never know when they'll come," she'd say.

I followed her instructions then, and still do today. Upon waking, I say this little prayer: "Divine Mother, Father, and

God, I'm grateful for your presence in my life. Joy guides, I'm grateful for your presents throughout my day. Thank you."

I love playing with them and letting them bring me many gifts. Once when visiting my sister in Kansas, we took my mother's advice and went out to lunch, both of us actually expecting presents. We waited an unusually long time to be seated at the good restaurant we'd chosen. But we were so engaged in conversation that we didn't even notice the time. Finally, the manager did notice, and she apologized and gave us each a gift certificate for a free dinner!

Happy with our good fortune, we strolled next door to an apparel shop. My sister found a beautiful pair of pants that fit perfectly, but had a tiny bit of dirt on them—nothing a dry cleaner couldn't take care of. She showed the pants to the owner, who apologized and said, "If you buy something else, I'll just give you these pants. It's the end of the season and not worth the expense of cleaning." My sister chose a blouse and left with a complete outfit.

Outside, we found two teenagers washing the car. When we asked what they were doing, they said that it was community-service day. We offered to pay, but they refused the money. We laughed and sang all the way home—thank you, joy guides!

Your Turn

Summon your joy guides every day. Give them names. Appreciate their antics. Ask them for presents and help them to help you by remembering that nothing is worth losing your sense of humor. If you aren't sure what kind of present you want to receive, then say "Surprise me." They will. They're the bridge to heaven.

Chapter 19

Light Beings

Last April when I was in Kauai with my team of healers and helpers presenting Translucent You, a six-day intensive workshop designed to heal our clients on a deep soul level, a new and very powerful source of guidance made contact. I first became aware of this intense, new spirit force on the afternoon of the third day, as I met with the group of 30 for an afternoon meditation.

Relaxing to the beautiful music created by my musician friend Mark Welch, I instructed the class to gently close their eyes and concentrate on their breathing as it flowed into and out of their bodies. Moments later, I lost all awareness of the group as I suddenly saw in my mind's eye what appeared to be an army of tall, blue, cylindrical beings approaching me with open arms and an intense amount of love. Their vibration was so high that I became completely absorbed by their powerful healing energy.

Slowly I felt my head tip back and my ego awareness step aside as this throng of Light Beings approached and then burrowed into my body to speak to the group through what's known as channeling. I was conscious, but felt far removed from my own physical self, as though I were watching from some faraway place, as fascinated by what was happening as everyone else.

The creatures introduced themselves as the Emissaries of the Third Ray and respectfully asked for permission to address the group. Not sure what was occurring, but sensing the same intense vibration of deep love that I felt radiating through me, the group agreed.

Then the Light Beings began to share a clear and urgent message. Through me, they began by telling us how loved and precious we all are, but how we must change our vibration from one of fear to love if we hope to survive as individuals and as the human race. With great compassion, the Emissaries said that they were connecting through me to them (and back to me) to offer their assistance in helping us achieve this transformation. As they spoke through me, my voice took on an entirely different tone and cadence than my own. It was strange but not uncomfortable.

I was struck by how powerful their vibration felt as it coursed through my being. Their light and love was so great that it felt as if 10,000 watts of energy were channeling through a 200-watt circuit and threatening to blow me apart at any moment. Incredibly, what happened instead was that my heart opened to a degree I'd never felt before.

I felt intoxicated because I was so high on this wave of love. Every cell in my body felt energized and renewed; aches and stiffness gave way to absolute peace and calm; all the worry and anxiety in my history yielded to perfect ease. With the assistance of these loving Light Beings, I felt at one with the Universe and with God.

They only spoke for a few moments, but talking wasn't the most important thing. They conveyed such a tremendous healing vibration that words couldn't possibly communicate their message, and I later found out that everyone present felt the same way. By transmitting this powerful vibration of love, the Emissaries of the Third Ray expanded our heart chakras to a much wider level than any of us thought possible. We got the message because we felt it.

After channeling through me for several minutes, they receded, thanking us for our attention and telling us that to feel their presence again, all we had to do was open our hearts and let them flow through our hands. Then slowly I returned to my own consciousness.

I'd channeled guides before, allowing them to speak through me, especially the Three Bishops, my teacher guides, but never before had I gone into such a deep, altered state or felt so physically affected.

After they left, we all sat in astounded silence. We all felt the shift in energy and the exhilarating freedom from fear. This vibration of full, loving power was so radically different from the frequency of consciousness we were accustomed to that we were speechless. There was no need to say anything . . . we were in bliss.

This first contact with the Emissaries was quite exciting. For the past five years, I'd been feeling them trying to come through, but my vibration wasn't open and grounded enough for them to connect until then. I wondered if I'd be able to make contact again, and so did the rest of the group.

The next day at our afternoon meditation session, the Emissaries of the Third Ray returned. As their unbelievably high vibration filled me with light and affection, it nearly knocked me off my feet. This time, a spokesman stepped forward from this blue army of love and introduced himself as Joachim.

He greeted us with the same respect and affection as the Emissaries had before and asked our permission to speak. It was eagerly granted, and through me he began to convey what was again called an urgent message. Speaking slowly, deliberately, and with tremendous intention, he told us that the human race won't survive unless we shift our fundamental consciousness away from merely getting by. He said that the planet won't be able to support the levels of fear we're creating, and that great numbers of people consumed by terror would need to leave Earth in order to rebalance it.

He related that this wouldn't necessarily happen if everyone shifted their survival energies from fear and withholding to loving and giving. They'd not only be fully protected and safe in this time of change, but would also be the progenitors of a new race of higher beings. As he spoke, I again felt the profound peace and calm I had the day before, and so did the group.

Using my body and my hand, Joachim then demonstrated how to generate this powerful heart-chakra energy. He asked everyone present to open their hearts and extend their hands outward, intending a vibration of love to pour through them and into the world. Thus, he assured us, we could create and attract whatever we desired.

Feeling a potent vibration running through my being when I followed this instruction (as did others, I found out later), I understood how what he said could be true. This unrestrained flow of caring that the Emissaries of the Third Ray were helping each of us channel into the world was so compelling and peaceful that I intuitively knew it was the same vibration Christ had used to heal. If we tapped in to this fully and called it home, then we, too, could perform miracles.

Joachim said that the Emissaries had come to help us usher in the miracle of unrestrained love that the world desperately needed right now. Then he and the other Light Beings led us in a heart-opening meditation that put us in an altered state for hours. We were told that having our minds quieted and our hearts opened was the beginning of a new kind of human, and they were here to show us how to plant those seeds.

With a final blessing, Joachim withdrew, but not before assuring us that the Emissaries of the Third Ray and many other armies of Light Beings are available at all times to guide anyone ready to release fear and move into the vibration of love.

Joachim and the Emissaries have been strongly connected to me ever since. They told me that my spirit has agreed to be one of the midwives of the new emerging type of human beings, who will be rooted in love, not fear. My mission is to help people activate and expand their heart chakra and become energetically rooted in its caring. I believe it, because ever since I was a child I've been preparing for this. Now the Emissaries come through in all my public appearances to help me activate this higher vibration in everyone present. They—and other Light Beings—are contacting many others who are open to shifting the earth to love, because without a great deal of cooperation, we won't succeed.

Did You Know That Light Beings . . .

. . . tell us that the Universe has a spiritual plan to ultimately raise the vibration of the earth to a higher octave of harmony and balance?

. . . are connecting with us more than ever before in order to bring greater understanding and love to us as we face the important changes now taking place?

. . . assist us as the earth purges itself of old negative patterns that have accumulated in our confusion?

. . . will guide us through these changing times?

Perhaps you've been contacted. You'll know you have if you suddenly feel a deep and urgent need to forgive all ego-based hurt feelings and past injuries and choose to love yourself, others, and life with your heart and soul.

You may not have had the same direct connection as I have, but you can and will be reached if you feel called upon to do your part in fulfilling their mission. As this occurs, your heart eases and you begin to feel the life and spirit we all share. You can never again look at another person and feel separate or any sort of hatred or judgment. This doesn't mean that you won't have your moments or get upset or irritated. It just means that these feelings and fear-based vibrations will no longer be important enough to hold on to.

Initially, I hesitated to share my connection with the Emissaries of the Third Ray so early in my experience with them, but they encouraged me to do so, as their message is important: "Move away from fear as your root energy and embrace love in its place." I feel the urgency of this information and hope that you do, too.

Your Turn

Open your heart to the Light Beings and let them into your vibration—it's that easy. Ask for their help whenever you feel fear directly or in the form of anger, judgment, sadness, or any of its other disguises. With a slow breath, open your heart and extend your hands. At first it may feel as if nothing is happening, but don't be discouraged. Continue to breathe, and keep your center open.

You'll soon feel their support, as their kindly forces are very strong. Try it right now and see if you sense them. If so, enjoy their healing vibration; if not, continue to breathe and release your fear.

Whether you feel it or not, the Light Beings are present. On a personal level, they'll inspire a profound sense of peace no matter what's going on in your life. On a cosmic level, you'll join the forces that want us to love ourselves and save this beautiful planet. I do hope that you'll join me and others in this effort.

Chapter 20

Negative Entities

When opening up to your spirit guides, it's very important to be grounded and discriminating so that you attract and engage high-vibration guides who will assist your life— and not low-vibration, negative entities that only disturb and distort things and cause trouble.

Just as you wouldn't invite a stranger into your home and give him a measure of control, you shouldn't accept that all guides are useful or worthwhile without some initial scrutiny. Most are wonderful Light Beings, but there are some spirits that aren't of a high vibration. They're wandering around lost and confused and would love to grab you and try to run your life instead of floating aimlessly through the ether. Most of these lesser spirits are harmless but annoying and can be easily recognized by their vibration.

High-vibration guides are subtle, patient, calm, loving, and don't tell you what to do. Instead, they make subtle suggestions, usually upon request, and leave you feeling peaceful and supported. Low-vibration entities, on the other hand, are pushy, bossy, negative, and will do everything in their power to control you, including flattering you, criticizing others, or psychically harassing you into doing what they want, which is to create drama and trouble.

They'd like you to believe that they're mighty forces that you must obey, but they really have no power and can be easily dismissed. To do so, you need only send them into the light with your intention and firmly ask them to leave. They're mostly nuisances who entertain themselves at your expense, and they sneak into your field of awareness when you aren't grounded or focused.

You can also identify low-vibration entities because they're very seductive. They suggest things to make you feel more important, smart, or special than others. A high-vibration guide would never do that because it knows that on a spirit level we're all the same, although unfolding at different rates of consciousness. No one is special, because we're all connected. Entities speak to your ego; higher guides connect with your spirit.

These energies like to blame others for your problems and encourage you to feel victimized and sorry for yourself; they want you to keep your distance from others. Trustworthy guides, on the other hand, encourage you to look at your challenges and experiences as soul lessons, seeing that whoever or whatever is involved is only helping you learn to grow spiritually. They ask you to lovingly study and learn from all situations, and once the lesson is learned, to move on. They don't play the blame game, and they support you in viewing others with compassion and forgiveness.

Negative entities boss you around and hound you. Eager to wield influence, they have a harassing feel about them, which is in contrast with high-vibration guides, who are quite subtle and enter your world slowly and respectfully, and only when asked.

What Attracts Negative Entities

Fear of these beings scares many people from opening up to guides, turning them away from their profound spiritual resources. It isn't all that easy to attract low-vibration entities, but even if you do, they can be easily eliminated. Nevertheless, it's useful to know what things *do* attract them so that you can avoid this nuisance altogether.

Perhaps the most obvious attraction is addiction of any sort, from alcoholism to workaholism. It weakens your aura, confuses your will, disturbs your spirit, and sabotages your creativity. It creates chaos in your energy field, much like having an invader in your home. When you're addicted, you're out of control, so it should come as no surprise that negative entities seize the opportunity to enter. The way to shut that door is to acknowledge the problem and treat it.

Another attraction is being chronically passive and unfocused in your priorities and goals. That doesn't mean that you must know what you want to do at every moment, but you need to at least be clear about what you value in order to keep from drifting into negative territory. If you're the type of person who wants to be led around by the nose and take no responsibility for your life, low entities will take advantage of you, just as people will.

Also, Universal law states: "Like attracts like." If you're angry, judgmental, aggressive, jealous, and mean-spirited, you'll pull in the same qualities on the unseen level. I'm not talking about having a bad moment or one episode of unpleasantness—that's human. I mean being chronically negative, an entirely different vibration that attracts low-entity energy.

If you're extremely run-down, very stressed, or in an emotionally weakened state, there's the slight possibility that you may pick up a negative entity in a public place, just as you would a cold. For example, I've had them attach to me on airplanes and in hotel rooms, restaurants, and even hospitals. These irksome energies lurk wherever there's a "down" or stressful vibration over a long period of time. Like stowaways, they grab on to higher vibrations such as you and tag along. They usually don't mean harm; they're just trying to get out of the limbo they're in.

Did You Know That

Negative Entities. . .

. . . encourage you to be judgmental and critical of everyone and everything?

. . . are very weak energies and can never overwhelm the human spirit?

Signs of a negative entity hanging around are suddenly falling into a very bad or irritable mood, snapping at people, feeling surges of self-doubt or a loss of energy, and viewing the world in depressed or cynical terms, especially when this isn't your normal behavior.

Hollywood has attempted to frighten us with its version of these beings and what occurs when they're present, but don't be fooled. Not only is what you see on the silver screen a fantasy, it's also absurd. They're simply like flies coming into the light—not the *Night of the Living Dead.* And just for the record, I've never seen an entity possess anyone. They may give you a scare, but the human spirit is pretty strong and not easily diminished.

Banishing Negative Entities

Generally, negative entities are dispelled the minute you enter positive energy. However, if you suspect that you've attracted one, don't be frightened. It's no different from a virus, and if you catch it early, it can be easily tossed aside by simply raising your vibration with positive thoughts of things and people you love.

If an entity has been attached to you for a while or is particularly tenacious, you may need to perform a ritual to get rid of it. Begin by asking your angels and archangels to clear your aura of all negative forces. Next, take a long Epsom-salt bath to get rid of any lingering psychic debris. Finally, request that your Higher Self remove any remaining unpleasant energies and say aloud: "I send all negative entities into the light now. I am free and clear of all psychic debris." That ought to do the job—it does for me.

I do find that the people who tend to attract negative entities the most are those who have weak and unhealthy boundaries. Just as leaving the doors and windows to your home open all the time might attract burglars, having your aura open can result in psychic intruders. High-vibration guides would never trespass upon your boundaries, even when they're shaky or not strongly in place, but low-vibration beings will and do.

To establish healthy limits, simply say out loud: "I claim my life, my boundaries, and my right to be fully myself at all times. I invite only the highest support to connect with my heart, in both the physical and nonphysical world. I am protected from any influence that doesn't serve my highest good." And mean it when you say it.

Practice not taking on what isn't your responsibility. If someone isn't feeling positive, then send them love, but don't absorb their vibration. If necessary, simply step away from their bad vibes. Put up a white light in your mind's eye, and let it serve as a shield to block all negativity.

Establish clear boundaries when asking for guidance or opening your psychic channels. Similar to a filter designed to remove debris, setting boundaries before asking for guidance is smart. To do so, request that only the most loving guides be allowed to enter and influence your energy. That's enough to prevent a problem.

On a rare occasion, a nastier entity may latch on and cause havoc. I've seen it happen, and it's disturbing. Like psychic brats who refuse to respect you, some of these creatures will test you. I've witnessed this especially with teenagers on drugs and bored, noncommittal, unfocused people who are hoping to spice up their lives with a little psychic excitement.

Even at this level, these entities can be dispelled if those being bothered ask for help, surround themselves with their own prayers, ask others to pray for them, and reset their intention to their most important goals of the moment. If you believe that someone is troubled by an entity, you can dispel it for him or her by asking it to leave now and enter the light in the name of God. It must obey, as there's nothing greater than God.

Don't spend a lot of time discussing these beings, because they're fed by talk. Like hooligans playing tricks, they love to scare people and thrive on attention. Instead of falling prey to this, insist that they leave, which will dispel their meager power quickly.

I've written about entities because they're a nuisance and can cause trouble, but you shouldn't regard them as a big problem. Just be discriminating when opening your psychic channels, and have some sound boundaries in place. If you're clear and grounded and remember to surround yourself with Divine light and protection, you'll be okay.

Your Turn

If you do encounter an entity, follow these steps:

- Stay grounded.

- Draw your boundaries.

- Call in your angels and archangels to clear your aura.

- Take an Epsom-salt bath.

- Ask for help and for others to pray for you.

- Recommit to your goals.

This should eliminate your problem, and better yet, you can take these steps as a preventive measure to keep one from occurring.

Now that you've become familiar with specific guides and their purpose in your life, let's move on and learn how to comfortably recognize how they work with us.

PART V

Working Directly with Your Spirit Guides

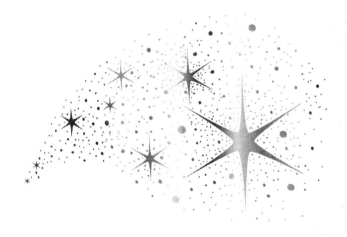

Chapter 21

Your Spirit Guides Are Closer Than You Think

Now that you've been introduced to many of the types of spirit guides that are available to you, it's time to discuss exactly how you're supposed to work with them. I'm convinced that the greatest obstacle to receiving wisdom from them on a regular basis is simply being misinformed about how they're supposed to communicate with you. I can't emphasize enough the subtlety of spirit guides and how easy their signs are to miss or dismiss.

And yet, I must also say that once you've invited them to assist you, they'll seize each moment and use every means possible to get your attention. It's simply a matter of recognizing their efforts and appreciating how close and committed to communicating with you they are.

One of the most consistent ways in which your guides connect to you is through inspiration. They're the ones who inspire you with an idea, solution, new course of action, or some means of creative expression. The word *inspiration* is taken directly from the word *spirit,* so when you're in this state, you're communicating with these assistants.

A talented singer and songwriter client of mine named Claire came to me with this great story: She said that when she was in college, she studied abroad in France, as I did. Feeling very lonely and out of place on one cold, dreary December day, she considered leaving. As she planned her withdrawal, she was inspired to take the Metro home from school rather than walking the six short blocks, as she'd routinely done in the past to save money.

The inspiration hit as she found herself in front of a Metro stop. She decided to get on a train without hesitation, not even sure that it was the right line. As she descended the stairs to the station, she heard beautiful music being played by a group of young men singing at the top of their lungs in English, which made her smile for the first time in quite a while. Taken by the music and their energy on such a gloomy day, she went to the platform and found three extremely cute guys playing guitars with their cases open for tips. They began chatting, and she learned that two of them, Jay and Skip, were from London, and the third, Tony (whom she found very attractive), was from New Zealand.

To her delight, they asked if she wanted to stay and sing with them, and they even offered to share the tips. Having nothing else to do, she agreed. The next thing she knew, six hours had passed, and she'd had the time of her life. She made plans to meet them again the next day. This went on every day for the remainder of the school year—during which she stayed, finished her classes, and fell in love with Tony. They got married and moved back to New Zealand, where they started a record company producing their own CDs.

The even wilder part of this story, she said, was that she never even knew that she liked singing! This all happened, she marveled, simply because she followed her inspiration to take the Metro instead of walking.

Another client, Jacob, by training a creative director in advertising but a musician in his heart, followed a traditional path in life. He went to work right after college for an ad agency and stayed at the same job for 25 years. He married, lived in the Chicago suburbs, and had two children.

His love of music sat dormant, staring him in the face every day and leaving him sad. Torn between his role as a father, husband, and provider and his secret desire to be a blues musician, he became very depressed over the years.

Then one day he got the inspiration to approach the owner of a restaurant where he and his family often ate and propose a musical family night on the weekends. He suggested an evening where he and a few other musicians could play; and families could come and enjoy the music, eat, dance, and have fun. Although he thought it was a long shot, he followed his inspiration anyway.

The owner was enthusiastic, and the first night was so successful that Jacob was invited to be a regular. Neighboring restaurants called to request him as well, and in no time a weekend business was born. He didn't even have to quit his day job.

Did You Know That Spirit Guides . . .

. . . work behind the scenes dropping great ideas into your awareness in the form of inspiration?

. . . may not provide inspiration through the channels that you expect?

To recognize and act on your inspirations requires an open mind. Spirit guides can offer the best assistance to those who are willing to help themselves. They provide inspiration, but it's up to you to accept it and do something with it.

For example, 20 years ago, Patrick, an avid bicyclist, had a sudden inspiration to import and sell French and Italian bicycle jerseys and shorts in the U.S., where they were virtually unknown. I thought it was a terrific plan and encouraged him to look into it right away. But he only pursued it as far as a good friend who said that it was a ridiculous idea because American men would never wear spandex, so Patrick dropped the idea.

Two years later, spandex flooded the American market, with French and Italian bicycle jerseys being big sellers. Patrick was given the inspiration but rejected it; it was obviously passed on to someone else who ran with it.

Patrick is not an isolated case. In my practice as a psychic, I constantly hear clients who complain to me that "someone stole my idea." The truth is, no one took anything. It's just that your spirit guides will inspire you with a concept whose time has come, but if you ignore it, it will be taken to another open-minded soul who will accept and use it. I can't tell you how many times I've heard people bemoan being members of the "woulda, coulda, shoulda" club of missed opportunity and intuitive breakthroughs because they chose to ignore their inspiration.

Some of the greatest music, art, literature, and even scientific breakthroughs were inspired by guides and received openheartedly. So start paying attention to your inspiration today; more important, see what you do with those gifts of the spirit. Do you see them as presents delivered by your guides and therefore put them to use? Or do you dismiss them as crazy notions and stay in your same rut?

As I ask you this, I'm reminded of the joke where a man worked tirelessly for the church, believing that God would always take care of and protect him. One year there was a terrible flood in his town. Everyone evacuated, but he stayed, saying that God would provide. Soon the first floor of the church was underwater, and a car showed up to rescue him, but he stayed, saying that he trusted in the Lord.

The water rose higher, so he ran to the choir loft, and the next thing he knew, the entire church was underwater. A boat arrived to save him, but he stayed put, saying the same thing and running to the roof, where a helicopter soon hovered above him and dropped a ladder. He refused the ladder, and he drowned.

In heaven, he angrily accosted God and asked, "Why didn't you take care of and protect me?" To which God answered, "What do you mean? I sent you a car, a boat, and a helicopter!"

I tell this joke because it's close to the truth of how the higher forces connect with us. They'll capture our attention once, twice, or even more. My teacher Charlie once said, "If it crosses your mind twice, it absolutely is; more than that and your guides are nearly screaming at you." In other words, help from the spirit world is available, but it comes in its own way and not necessarily how you expect it to.

Your Turn

If you want to benefit from your spirit helpers, pay attention to how your guides work, and don't refuse their help just because they don't do things your way.

Accept every inspiration, impulse, and bright idea as an important message from above, and don't waste time arguing, dismissing, or questioning it . . . or you may miss that last helicopter.

Chapter 22

Guides Work with Messengers, Too

The intent of guides to get your attention can be impeded by your emotional state. If you're stressed, worried, or are experiencing any kind of emotional upheaval, it's nearly impossible for your guides to directly get through. And face it—this is when you need them most.

So what do your guides do? Rather than trying to communicate with you or inspire you directly, they will often engage the help of someone around you to deliver their supportive messages. In fact, chances are that someone else's guides have used you to help one of their charges as well.

For example, have you ever felt compelled to pick up the phone for no reason and just call someone who tells you that you couldn't have possibly called at a better time? My client Jeff told me recently that he was on his way to his construction job at 6 A.M. last spring when he had the overwhelming urge to call his grandmother, whom he loved, but hadn't spoken to in more than a year. His feeling was so strong that in spite of the early hour, he called her right then. She answered, crying.

"Are you okay?"

"Oh, Jeff, I thought you were the vet, and no, I'm not okay. My cat Bob just died. He's been my best friend and companion for the past 20 years. Now I have no one. I feel just terrible."

Devastated by her grief, Jeff said, "I'm so sorry, Gram. But you're wrong about one thing. You're not alone. I'm free this weekend, and I'm coming to see you. Hang in there, Gram. I'll be there late this evening to help you get through this." He left right after work.

Another client, Jesse, told me that she was sitting quietly one morning at a Starbucks working on a report for her job when, quite out of character, she asked the woman sitting at the next table if she were a regular.

The woman said, "Actually, no. Well, yes. Well, no. What I mean is, I just moved here from Indiana, and I've only been here for three days. I'm staying with my roommate from college, and I'm looking for an apartment in this neighborhood. I'd love to live here, but I've been told it's really hard to find something at this time of year."

Jesse laughed and said, "This is so strange. My landlord asked me this morning if I knew anyone looking for an apartment. She didn't want to go through the hassle of advertising. I've lived there for five years and love it. It's only three blocks from here. Here's her number."

The woman signed a lease before lunch. The two women became great friends. The woman's guides had borrowed Jesse to help their charge.

As another example, consider my dear friend Bill. A Chicago television host and a bachelor who wanted very much to meet his heart's desire, he could hardly believe it when one day he got his wish. A beautiful woman, Angela, had come to interview him for a local magazine. The chemistry was undeniable. Yet, fearing it wasn't real, he asked his spirit helpers for some kind of sign to let him know that love was truly in the air as he walked from work to meet her for lunch.

When he entered the restaurant, the maître d' gave him a rose. When he asked what it was for, the man said, "I don't know. Something told me to give this to you." Imagining the rose to be the sign he had asked for, Bill took it, and at the table he offered it to Angela. A year later, they were married.

"The rose clinched it," said Bill. "When I received that rose, I knew that my wish was about to come true. And it did."

Did You Know That . . .

. . . every message that catches your attention has meaning, no matter who the messenger is?

Your Turn

Reflect on a time when you were the spontaneous messenger and guide for someone, a time when you called just in time to save someone's day, said the right thing, or offered the right solution. What happened? When did it happen? How did it happen? Who was involved? What was the outcome? Did you feel the influence of the Other Side in this event? Tell at least one interested person about this experience, and notice the effect it has on you.

In those situations, the other person's guides borrowed you for a moment and used you to deliver a helpful message. That's the beauty of this infinitely loving Universe. We're all interrelated and can be helped and helper at the same time.

Chapter 23

Spirit Speak

In addition to being subtle, instead of speaking to us in direct language, spirit guides can use riddles, metaphors, symbols, dreams, and even jokes to speak to us. So not only must you become adept in picking up on subtle vibrations, you must also recognize that the spirit world has its own language, and it's up to you to learn it.

Don't let this scare you. Your guides don't want to trick or confuse you. In fact, their method of communication is often clearer, stronger, and more humorous than a direct message.

I had a client, a flight attendant, who had a real sweet tooth. One morning at 4 A.M., as she was preparing to make the 40-mile trek to the airport, she heard in her mind, "Isn't it a good day for doughnuts?"

Used to talking to her guides and loving the thought of a fresh doughnut, she said out loud, "Yes, but I'm running late. I can't stop this morning."

Putting her bag into the car, she heard it again. "Isn't it a good day for doughnuts?" Laughing, she said "Yes, it is. But I can't stop. I'm late." Just as she was about to drive onto the highway from the access road, she saw a doughnut truck pulling into the gas station next to the turnoff.

Again her guides piped in. "Isn't it a good day for doughnuts?"

"All right, I give up. But I have to hurry." Pulling in to the service station behind the doughnut truck, she turned off the ignition and saw that she was just about out of gas. She gasped as she realized that she could have run out on the highway and missed her flight altogether. The guides said in unison: "See, isn't it a good day for doughnuts?"

My client Fred was in the shower one morning getting ready for work when he heard, "Get out of the fast lane." He imagined that it was a metaphoric message from his guides to slow down and take it easy. He was soon to learn it was much more. On the road for his 25-mile commute, he entered the fast lane as he always did. He instantly blew out his front right tire and nearly lost control of the car.

"Fortunately, I held on to the wheel and maneuvered out of the fast lane and crossed three more lanes to the side of the road without getting hit or hitting someone else," he told me. "It was a miracle. I got out of the car, inspected the tire, and saw the thinnest shred of rubber dangling off the rim. Then I remembered what I'd heard in the shower. I said to my guides gratefully, 'I guess you weren't mincing words today.'"

He said that as he started walking toward the exit ramp seeking help, he looked down and saw a nickel and a penny. Bending to pick them up, he said aloud, "Oh, six cents." It dawned on him that his guides were having a little fun with him.

"Six cents. Sixth sense. I get it. Thank you again. Now please send help."

Learning spirit speak is a trial-and-error process that requires patience and a sense of humor. Guides love laughter and try to make you laugh. The more you do so, the higher your vibration, and they love to feel this vibe from you, so they play with you whenever they can.

I was teaching a class on communicating with your guides at the Omega Institute in New York, and as an exercise paired up the students and invited the class to try speaking to their guides directly. Expecting profound revelations, one frustrated student raised her hand. "I'm not getting this at all. All I hear from my guides is 'Jelly beans. Tell your partner to have fun with jelly beans.' And that's just ridiculous."

The minute she said that, the student she was working with gasped and said, "Oh, my God! Why did you say that? I've been wondering all morning if I should get a new puppy to fill up the loneliness in my life because the woman who lives next door offered me one from her dog's new litter. His name is Jelly Beans! So I guess that answers my question."

Sometimes your guides come to you in symbols. A client who was constantly bombarded with images of butterflies asked me why. "My neighbor just called me up and asked me if I wanted a butterfly tree for my birthday. I didn't even know there was such a thing."

I suggested that every time she encountered a butterfly over the next six months, she should write down in her journal exactly what was going on. Once she started documenting the appearance of butterflies, she realized that they showed up within one hour of her asking the Universe and her guides for reassurance that she was on the right life path. They were her guides communicating that all was well.

Another woman in one of my classes told me that every time she was about to make a mistake, Elton John's song "Don't Let the Sun Go Down On Me" popped into her head. The last time she heard it, she had just gotten engaged to a man she was crazy about—or at least she was crazy about his looks and his money (he was a handsome professional athlete). When she got in her car the next day, she turned on the radio and heard Elton John singing the song.

She screamed and turned it off, but she knew that it was a sign that all was not okay. After a very turbulent six-month engagement, they called it off. One of the last things he said to her during a stupid fight was, "And another thing—I hate Elton John."

One way your guides choose symbols is to work with those that you've already connected with. For example, when my daughter Sonia was very young, she loved the book *The Runaway Bunny.* Whenever she was acting out, I'd ask her if she was my runaway bunny. When she became a teenager and was testing limits, every time she'd drift to the edge of acceptable behavior, a bunny of some sort would appear.

Once when she was considering lying about a sleepover and going to a concert we felt she was too young to attend, a bunny ran in front of her just outside her school door. She asked us instead, and my husband and I agreed she could attend as long as we drove her to and from the show. Another time, after a huge mother-daughter argument, she stormed out, went for a walk, and saw two rabbit's feet in separate places. She came back and apologized. In the meantime, a wooden rabbit in my office fell off the shelf for no apparent reason. I apologized to her as well. And when she was considering taking a trip with a friend she wasn't sure she wanted to spend that much time with, Patrick emerged from the basement with Sonia's original tattered copy of *The Runaway Bunny* and gave it to her. She stayed home.

So what gets your attention? If you can't answer this immediately, don't worry. Just plant this question in your awareness and let the answer come.

A client who was just beginning to work with signs and symbols shared this interesting story: One day, just as she was about to go shopping with a girlfriend, she heard her guides say, "Can't go until you shuffle your cards." She thought, *What a funny idea,* and dismissed it as she continued to get ready. A few seconds later, she heard it again, this time in a playful voice. It dawned on her that maybe the guides were referring to the brand-new deck of tarot cards she'd just purchased and had looked at earlier that morning. Not wanting to shuffle her cards just then, she ignored the message, grabbed her purse, and moved toward the door.

Again she heard loud and clear, "Can't go until you shuffle your cards." She suddenly smelled something funny. She looked at the closed glass door to her office and saw that the room was filled with smoke. She opened the door and found a glass votive candle still burning that she'd lit earlier.

The glass had become so hot that it was now causing the table to smolder. She blew out the candle and snuffed out the burning embers.

"This could have burned the house down," she said aloud. Then she saw that right next to the candle was her deck of cards. Grateful to her guides for the warning, she picked up the deck and shuffled. "Thank you," she said. "Let me know anytime when you want me to shuffle the cards." Then a card dropped from the deck. It was the ace of hearts, which means "You are protected by love."

Once you begin connecting consciously to the unseen world, you can learn to speak its language. It's full of symbols, scents, riddles, jokes, and even sounds—all of which are selected to mean something to you. Approach the spirit world as you would an exotic foreign land—admire its scenery, enjoy its native customs, and accept the hospitality of its inhabitants, your spirit guides. Before you know it, you'll be fluent in their language.

Did You Know That . . .

. . . part of learning to communicate with your guides is to become fluent in the subtle art of symbols and signs, and respond to them when they show up? The more you recognize them, the more they'll make sense to you.

Your Turn

In a small pocket notebook, start keeping track of objects, impulses, images, phrases, melodies, ideas, and even random thoughts that seem to pop up unexpectedly and recurrently in your life. After two weeks, look back though your notes. Is there a pattern? Do you recognize any further meaning or any hidden humor within these messages now that some time has passed? Is someone trying to tell you something? Pay attention, and notice what's trying to come through.

Chapter 24

Your Guides' Names

One of the most popular questions clients ask me is, "What is my guide's name?" As I hope you know by now, you're connected during your life to many guides, not just one, and when they leave their physical bodies, most of them have no gender or name but exist on an energetic level. However, to help us better connect with them, they will sometimes take on a name and even a gender. They'll usually assume the identity in which they knew you in a past life in order to help you remember them, and reconnect with them on a conscious level.

Other guides, especially those from other solar systems or nonphysical frequencies, will simply assume a name that best replicates their vibration. Usually vowels and open sounds have a much higher frequency than consonants, which is why you hear of many guides whose names are airy, and light—Ariel, Abu, or some other short, open sound.

Some guides are loved ones, family members, or friends who have crossed over and may still be operating energetically in the same or similar frequency as when you knew them. So that you can recognize them, they often use their earthly name. When their name crosses your mind several times, you can be sure they're with you. When someone has recently passed, their name will obviously be on your mind extremely often. To tell whether this is just because they're recently departed or because they're trying to communicate with you, try to see if you sense their spirit or any other signal that may be connected to them when their names comes up. If you do, then it's most likely their spirit trying to contact you. If not, then you're probably thinking of them in the context of their recent death.

My client Edith was married for more than 40 years to Stanley, whom she loved very much and with whom she lived in upper Michigan. When he suddenly died of a stroke, Edith was inconsolable. Several weeks after the funeral, as Edith was barely regaining her composure, she felt Stanley's presence everywhere, but nowhere as strongly as on the back porch where he used to rock in his chair. She found a red cardinal sitting on the chair and said, "What are you doing on Stanley's chair?" The bird didn't move. She moved closer and said, "Why are you here?"

Edith remembered how much Stanley loved the birds, so the incident unnerved her a little. The next day she again felt Stanley's presence and was drawn to the back porch where she found the same red cardinal perched on the chair's arm.

Again, it didn't fly away.

This went on for ten days. Finally, Edith said to the cardinal, "Stanley, is that you trying to tell me something?" The bird didn't move. "Is that you, Stanley? Really?" Then she poured out her heart, feeling that the bird was Stanley and was listening to her.

The most important message she delivered to the bird was a poignant good-bye to her late husband, which she'd been unable to do because he'd died so suddenly. The bird flew away after that and never came back. But the connection was made; Stanley was present and helped Edith move on.

A client in a recent weeklong workshop wanted desperately to connect with one of her guides to ask for help with her marriage. The minute she asked its name, James popped into her mind, followed by "with blue eyes and a way with words." Suspicious that it was that easy, she asked James if he could give her another sign that she had his name right and was indeed connected to a healing force. What immediately popped into her mind was, "Write your husband a letter to communicate. Don't talk." She pondered that thought for the next several days and then followed James's advice. She wrote her husband a ten-page letter explaining exactly what she wanted to change in their relationship, as well as what it was working for her, and asked him to do the same. Then she mailed it.

Two days later, while she was still at the workshop, he sent flowers and a return letter saying how much better he understood her, and agreed to work on the issues she had raised—all this from a man who normally stonewalled her verbally and emotionally. So James was her guide's name, she decided, and he more than proved himself to be a healing force, given the suggestions he offered.

Sometimes you won't get one name because you aren't working with one guide. As I mentioned earlier, I connect with three guides who speak as a trio and call themselves the Three Bishops. I'm also in contact with the Pleaidean Sisters, two beautiful angels who sometimes can be three or more, and they, too, speak to me in unison.

My dear friend Julia Cameron, when working on a movie years ago, wrote to her guides often, and they always answered in the plural without revealing their names. Another friend calls her guides the Light Ones.

Sometimes guides will give you a name through automatic writing. When connecting in this way, ask your guide or guides, "How shall I address you?" and see what flows from your pen.

The same goes for visualizing your guide in your sacred meeting place. When you see or sense a guide there, ask, "How shall I address you?" and listen for the answer.

If the name changes, it means that your guide has stepped back and another has taken its place, or your guide has shifted frequencies to a different vibration, creating a new name.

You can also *give* your guide a name. This doesn't change or modify the connection. The name you choose endears the guide to you, just as pet names or nicknames do. To quote Shakespeare in a scene from *Romeo and Juliet:* "What's in a name? That which we call a rose / By any other word would smell as sweet."

> *Did You Know That* . . .
>
> . . . the best way to find out a guide's name if it's not a friend or family member who has crossed over is to ask telepathically? Whatever comes to your minds first is the right name.

Your Turn

To connect with your guide's name, close your eyes and take a deep breath. Then ask your guide(s) to come forward. Once you sense your guide, ask, "How shall I address you?" Accept the first name that comes to mind. If no name comes, don't worry. Instead, name the guide yourself. Don't overthink. Have fun with this. Your guide will love the name you choose.

If you sense that you're connecting to a group of guides, ask their group name. Trust whatever comes through. Once you've established a name or names, request your guides by name every time you want to connect; you'll get a response. Assigning names does make the connections more personal and keeps the channels to high energy open even more. And choosing a particular name doesn't matter as much as sticking to it. Names are simply calling cards of intention. By being consistent, you forge strong connections and expand your ability to receive your guides' assistance. Enjoy your new supporters.

Chapter 25

Guides Help You— They Don't Do Your Work for You

It's extremely important to understand the role your guides play in your life if you want to have a positive experience with them. They love to assist and are never, ever bothered when you ask for their help. But they cannot—nor do they want to—do it all. I learned this for myself when my best girlfriend Lu Ann and I packed up my car in Chicago and set off for Denver in the middle of January when, after a year and a half on my own, I decided to move back home.

As I drove down the driveway, Lu Ann asked me if I had a map. "No," I arrogantly answered, "I don't need one. My guides will lead the way."

An hour later, stopping for gas, I realized that we were in Milwaukee, having gone 90 miles in the wrong direction. As the gas attendant laughed at me when I asked if we were on the right highway to get from Chicago to Denver, I humbly bought a map.

No matter who your guides are or what their level of expertise, when opening yourself to their influence it's important to understand that they're available to assist you, not to take over your life and run it. Their job is to lovingly provide clues and direction that will ease your cares and lead you to greater personal growth on your earthly journey. As tempting as it may be to desire a higher power to take over and save you from all potential mistakes, it would most likely become insufferable. After all, we're here to learn, and the only way to do so is by trial and error. Your guides don't want to do your work; they just want to help you learn your lessons as quickly and efficiently as possible while enjoying yourself.

In other words, don't get lazy (as I did that day) and think you can turn your life over to autopilot, not do your homework, and expect your guides to take over. High-level ones can't and won't take over. All they can do is support and assist you. Like the road map, they'll show you the best way to reach your goals, but they won't drive the car.

I must warn you, however, that there are low-level, earth-bound, and ego-bound entities who will gladly run your life if you allow them to. I had a client named Denise who sought the help of a guide because she'd acquired a lot of debt and wanted a quick fix. Rather than asking for help in learning how to better manage her money, she believed a spirit guide could simply make her some money and fast. The first question she asked her guide was if she should gamble at the new local riverboat casino to bring in quick cash, a plan another indebted friend had suggested.

Sure enough, a low-level entity piped right up and encouraged her to do just that. Convinced that she was being guided to win a fortune, she diligently went to the casino week after week on the advice of this reckless entity, in spite of the fact that each time she went she lost even more money. Not only did she not get out of debt as she'd hoped the guide would help her do, but she plunged more deeply into debt than ever. In six short weeks, she lost her house and had acquired more than $75,000 in credit-card debt over and above the $50,000 of debt she'd had to begin with.

Telling her shocked and shattered husband that her guide was to blame did her no good. It didn't relieve her predicament or save her assets—not to mention, it made her look like a nut. Rather than being honest and admitting that she had a problem, she blindly turned her power over to this entity, who manipulated her even into further trouble. She lost everything.

The best way to work directly with your guides is to ask for their assistance, but realize that at best they will make suggestions, through either gentle nudging, inspiration, or sudden insight. It's up to you to decide whether or not to listen and act upon their advice. No matter what is offered, use your good judgment and common sense and remember: Until you choose to act or not act, nothing will change.

Guides can't do things for you, change things for you, or make magic happen. They can only make you aware of the natural magic and benevolence of the Universe and urge you to align with it.

Here are four basic questions to help you decide whether the guidance you receive is worthwhile:

1. Is this guidance grounded and nonthreatening?
2. Does it feel gentle and loving?
3. Does it consider everyone involved?
4. Does it help me without harming anyone else?

If you can answer yes to all four of these questions, then the guidance you're receiving is worth considering. If you cannot, then the guidance is probably coming from a low-level source and not worth taking into consideration.

In any case, don't let any guidance distress you. If it's negative in the sense that it conveys information that you'd rather not hear, doesn't jive with your perspective, or disappoints you, listen anyway. Guides are not in the business of flattering you or agreeing with you. They *are* in the business of guiding you, which at times may be rough to listen to. If the guidance you get is negative in the sense that it suggests unloving things about you or others, makes you feel threatened or attacked, diminishes your spirit in any way, or encourages you to go against your better judgment, rather than let it frighten you, shrug it off and give it no importance whatsoever. Either you've unwittingly allowed an earthbound entity to slip into your awareness and play games with you or, more than likely, your own low self-esteem has taken on a louder-than-usual voice and is interfering with your spirit.

I spoke to a large crowd in Chicago recently, and while signing books I met with a very distressed young woman who said that her guide told her she and her best friend would soon die in a car accident and she wanted to know what I thought about that. I promptly told her I thought very little of such nonsense and that she should not waste another minute fretting about it. But I also told her that it didn't mean that she shouldn't be careful when driving. She was still obliged to use common sense whenever she got in a car. "Don't drink and drive. Don't speed. Obey the traffic rules, and pray for protection whenever you get in a car," I advised. "And relax. You just had a low-level entity scaring you for fun."

She seemed visibly relieved, and I was relieved for her. There was no point in her being tormented by something as toxic as being told of her imminent death. No worthwhile guide would ever do that. Death is a sacred communication between you and God, and guides do not interfere with that. Nor do high-level guides torment you or anyone with such frightening information. If she were really in danger, or even asking for trouble, her guide would warn her to drive more safely, not predict her death.

All high-vibration guides recognize you as a beautiful Divine spirit, beloved and precious, attending a very difficult and challenging classroom on Earth. They understand your challenges, have compassion for your struggles, and love and respect you very much. High-level guides feel privileged to assist you, and do so in a positive, respectful and compassionate way.

When speaking to your guides, don't ask them what you "should" do. Instead, ask them to guide you to your soul's highest good and help you make better-informed choices. By asking what you "should" do, you are in essence turning your power over to them, which they don't want you to do and will not accept. If you ask them to run your life in that manner, they become detached and remove themselves from your frequency, and you have to start all over connecting with them.

It's also important to recognize the difference between guidance and wishful thinking. True guidance is subtle and considers everyone, and will always lead you to the high road of personal responsibility, spiritual growth, and integrity. If you receive "guidance" that bypasses any of that, be suspicious. It's probably not so much guidance as your own ego talking, trying to trick you into being enslaved to its drives.

I had a client who asked her guide if she should get a divorce soon after meeting a handsome man who showed her some attention at a wedding. Unhappily married to an alcoholic, but also codependent and a shopaholic herself, she wanted an easy way out of her situation. Her guide was quiet, but her unhappy brain immediately said, "Yes, leave your husband because this new guy loves you." Convincing herself that she had met "Mr. Right" and had Divine permission to leave "Mr. Wrong," she filed the papers, ready to go after the new guy.

Shocked, her husband begged her not to proceed and even suggested marriage counseling, but she'd already set her sights on the wedding guest and wasn't interested. She was sure this was the right thing to do because her "guide" had said so.

The divorce went through quickly, and she pursued the new man, who promptly informed her that he had no genuine interest in her whatsoever and told her to "hit the road." She was devastated and confused. "My guide told me to get a divorce!" she cried in my office. "I trusted him. How could he mislead me so?"

"No guide would or can make that call," I assured her. "Are you sure it was your 'guide' and not your personal agenda?"

"I think it was my guide," she answered meekly. "It felt like my guide when it told me to leave my husband." But when I asked her the four basic questions, she couldn't reply yes to them.

"Then I believe it wasn't your guide," I mused, "because it wouldn't make that decision for you or be so insensitive to your husband. Maybe it wasn't a guide at all. Maybe it was you wanting an easy out."

"Maybe," she answered, thinking over the mess she had made of her life by acting so quickly without thinking things through. "Maybe."

A little clue in knowing when you're getting solid guidance or getting low-level input from your ego or low-vibration entities is that true guidance, even if it's not exactly what you were hoping to hear, always leaves you feeling satisfied and peaceful. It "pings" or energetically resonates deep within your body, and settles in and feels right, no matter what the message. If it's not solid guidance, it won't settle into your body. Instead, you'll find it rattling around your brain, like a loose ball bearing out of place. So listen to your body when it comes to guidance. Feel it rather than think about it, and soon you'll discern the difference.

Don't let the fear of low-vibration entities or the power of your ego prevent you from freely asking for assistance every time you're stuck. Your guides' purpose and intention is to help strengthen your direct connection to your highest good, and they're happy to help. The more you work with guides, the more your inner compass and intuition strengthens. This is one more clear indication that your guides are successfully working with you.

Did You Know
That a High-Level Guide . . .

. . . will *help* but not *run* your life?

. . . will inspire you but not make your decisions for you?

. . . makes subtle suggestions that harm no one?

. . . is never pushy?

. . . helps strengthen your intuition?

. . . leaves you feeling peaceful and supported?

Your Turn

To prevent any confusion when communicating with your guides and to distinguish between your guides and your ego, simply avoid the question "Should I . . ." altogether. Instead, ask, "Show me my best options." Then be patient and listen. By formulating questions in this way, the channel with your guides will keep strengthening and opening, and your ego and other undesirable energies will be silenced. Every time you ask "Should I . . . ," you're asking an outside force to take over. High guides refuse to do that; it's disrespectful. But your ego jumps in and will run the show if you let it.

It takes a little practice and attention to communicate correctly and with the right intention with your guides. Here's a little default trick that will keep you on the right path: Every morning say to your guides, "If I slip and say, 'Should I . . .' just know I really mean 'Show me my best options.'" That lets your guides know that you're not surrendering responsibility. You're just learning to be aware and may make mistakes. A week or two of this will most likely be enough to retrain you to ask for help correctly.

Chapter 26

Speaking to Your Guides Through Oracles

W hen I was 12 years old, I connected with my guides through my first oracle, an ordinary deck of playing cards. Although to most people they look like a simple tool to play games with, playing cards are actually descended from a numerological oracle handed down from the ancient civilization of Atlantis. Each card has a special meaning, which I learned from my mother while doing practice readings at our dining-room table.

At first, when working with the cards, it was all I could do to remember their meanings, but after a while something shifted and I moved beyond their basic meanings and felt that they were talking to me. When I began working with my psychic master teacher Charlie Goodman several years later, he told me that, indeed, my guides were talking to me through the cards. That made sense, because I was receiving far more than the basic meanings I'd learned.

I remember doing a reading for my best girlfriend (and mild skeptic at the time) Vicky. While staring at several cards, I distinctly felt that she was about to get a new car. Two days later her dad surprised her with a 1969 Road Runner. Although I spoiled the surprise, I was thrilled that I hadn't gotten Vicky's hopes up for nothing. She was, too, as we hot-rodded around Denver all that summer.

The more I did readings with my cards, the more I felt the guide who was working with me coming through. I eventually knew him as Joseph. The minute I'd pick up the deck and begin to shuffle, I would feel him beside me.

Cards are not the only way in which you can communicate with your guides. There are many oracles you can use. Whether they're tarot cards, pendulums, rune stones, the Chinese I Ching, or any of the other more modern versions of these ancient divination tools, all oracles create a direct link from your conscious mind to your Higher Self, your spirit, and all Divine forces in the Universe.

Oracles have been around for as long as humans have. Legend has it that the prehistoric cave drawings in central France were created by the ancient people of Lemuria as oracles of some sort to communicate with the heavens.

While you don't need to use oracles to communicate with your guides, they can make communicating with them a lot easier, in much the way that using training wheels makes learning to ride a bike easier. Just as it's quite possible to learn to ride without them, it's also possible to learn to communicate with your guides without oracles. But working with them does make the process, at least in the beginning, much more accessible.

There are many different types of oracles to choose from, and it's a matter of personal preference which one you're attracted to. There are rune stones, the Chinese I Ching, astrology, pendulums and of course, my all-time favorite, divination decks such as tarot cards. I think all oracles are wonderful because they provide extra avenues for your guides to communicate with you. Through oracles, the guides can point you in a certain direction, invite you to see things you've overlooked, warn you of inner digressions and outer threats, and remind you of what's important—all of which makes your spiritual journey much easier to travel.

Oracles work because they give your guides a language to use that you can understand, and when used properly, they work efficiently to connect you directly with your spirit guides and Higher Self.

Oracles are terrific tools to help you voice your guidance rather than merely have it rumble around in the back of your mind, muted and ignored. When working with oracles, the more you ponder their meanings out loud, the more guidance you tap in to from the higher realms.

My mother had a very dear psychic friend named Mary who used playing cards as her oracle. Her deck was so tattered from use over the years that I was sure the cards were going to fall apart in her hands every time she picked them up. When she did a reading, she shuffled until she felt her guides' presence, and only then would she begin. Mary, an old Hispanic Catholic, told me that her guides were St. Francis and St. Alphonsus. She read as soon as her "saints came marching in" by laying out the cards one at a time. She was very accurate; the cards for her revealed far more than their basic meanings.

Mary was the first person other than my mother to give me a reading using cards. She told me that her guides said I would be world famous one day. I was 13 years old at the time, so it was quite an incredible thing to hear. Staring at the same cards she was looking at, I asked which card said that. She shook her head and said it wasn't the cards themselves, but St. Francis who told her through the cards. I don't know if I can be called famous, but my books *have* become well known throughout the world, as St. Francis predicted. To this day, every time one of my books gets published in a foreign country, I thank St. Francis and think of Mary.

It's important when working with an oracle deck, or any oracle for that matter, not to repeat a question just because you didn't like the first answer. If you try to manipulate the oracle rather than allow it to reveal its wisdom freely, the guides retreat and the oracle loses its energy. It will simply not work for you.

This means, at its root, that to be successful with oracles, you need to be sincere and use common sense. Be willing to learn, and be respectful about what you get. My teacher Charlie said, "When you're spiritually mature, oracles work wonders and guide brightly through the night. When you're spiritually immature, they're possessed by low-level energies that mock you and make fun of you."

Many psychic and intuitive people are attracted to oracles other than playing cards as a means of connecting with their guides. I knew one woman, the late Hanna Kroeger, who lived in Boulder, Colorado, who was world famous for her ability to accurately diagnose and treat physical ailments with the use of her oracle, a pendulum on a chain. Holding the pendulum steady over a person, she could discern what the ailment was, both on a physical and emotional level, and recommend appropriate treatment.

My dear psychic friend and mentor of 30 years, Lu Ann (the same Lu Ann who went to Denver with me) often uses cards to connect with her guides. But even more useful and beloved by her is the I Ching, an ancient Chinese divination oracle. She consults it every morning to guide her during the day and uses it for readings. She keeps a journal of all her I Ching readings, and they've become a regular part of her morning conversation with her guides.

Lu Ann's best friend and my other mentor, Joan Smith, prefers using astrology as the oracle through which she connects with her guides. Although she relies on the charts alone for basic guidance, over time she's begun receiving assistance from her guides to help her hone in on very specific circumstances, events, and even dates that the charts are unable to determine. So, no matter what oracle or oracles you choose to explore and use, if you're sincere when consulting them, you'll receive wonderful guidance.

For reasons I don't fully understand, different oracles tend to attract different types of guides. The I Ching, rune stones, tarot, and divination cards tend to attract high-level guides who provide a great deal of direction and coaching.

The pendulum, however, can be hit or miss when it comes to the type of guide it attracts. Sometimes high-level guides come in, but sometimes low-level ones show up. I believe that's because a pendulum can easily be manipulated by the user's frame of mind and is therefore subject to confusion. That's not to say that a pendulum cannot be a great oracle to help you connect with your guides. Just know that it can be fickle, and it takes serious focus and concentration to attract the kind of guidance you desire when using it.

I'm a great fan of astrology and numerology, as they blend the use of higher logic with intuitive channels and can invite in the influence of wonderful guides if the practitioner is open to such input. It's quite possible, however, to approach both of these oracles without ever opening up your intuitive channels enough to intercept higher guidance, so while they can be, they're not necessarily a direct conduit to your spirit guides.

Did You Know That . . .

. . . tarot, the I Ching, astrology, numerology, pendulums, crystals, rune stones, *Ouija*, and divination decks are the most common oracles?

Your Turn

Whichever oracle you choose, just remember—these are tools to strengthen channels from your heart to your Higher

Self and guides. They're neutral, just like a phone. You dial in the inquiry, the Universe returns your call. The rules are simple:

- Get familiar and comfortable with your oracle.
- When applicable, protect it in a silk bag or purse.
- Don't let anyone else use it.
- Be sincere.
- Listen, learn, and discriminate.
- Don't ask the same question twice.
- Turn the final analysis over to your Higher Self.
- Enjoy yourself.

If you follow these basic rules, all oracles can be a powerful means to dialogue with your guides. Oracles have worked for me for the past 37 years, and I'm still learning from them.

If they attract you, try them. With the proper attitude and intention, they'll work for you, too. If you want to know more about oracles, there are many books on them, including information in my first book, *The Psychic Pathway*. As I said, it's not necessary to use oracles, but they're fun—especially divination decks, my personal favorite, which I will devote a little more discussion to in the next chapter.

Chapter 27

Oracle Divination Decks

Oracle divination decks such as the tarot are an excellent means of communicating with your guides. A divination deck usually consists of anywhere from 44 to 72 cards, depending on the deck, each one having a specific meaning that conveys a particular message to the questioner. Some divination decks, such as the classic tarot deck, are very sophisticated and complex and focus on growing one's soul, while others are much more basic, such as the Gypsy Witch Fortune Telling deck, and focus on simple and mundane matters such as, "Is my neighbor a friend?"

To use an oracle deck, all you have to do is shuffle while focusing on a specific question, issue, or even a specific person, and then pull cards at random and lay them out in predetermined patterns designed to address those questions, issues, or people.

There are literally hundreds of different oracle decks to choose from, including a regular deck of ordinary playing cards. Most decks are basically centered around the four elements: air, water, fire, and earth; and their corresponding physical, mental, emotional, and spiritual aspects.

Oracle decks have been around for a long time and have a rich history, dating back to the Middle Ages. Some decks have actually been in existence even longer and are rumored to come from Atlantis. Metaphysicians from times past preserved the spiritual teachings of the masters by creating a set of universally understood symbols and putting them in decks of cards that have endured in various forms to the present time.

The most traditional oracle deck is called a tarot deck and is usually divided into two groups, or arcana: 22 major and 56 minor cards, each representing a communication from your Higher Self and your guides. The major cards represent spiritual laws we all must learn; the minor cards represent the infinite ways in which we'll be asked to learn these laws.

The tarot contains a wealth of guidance and information, but it takes hard work to learn to use it. Each card has a specific symbolism and meaning. I've been studying tarot for more than 30 years and feel as though I'm only beginning to fully grasp the deepest meanings of the cards. However, you don't have to master and memorize the meanings in order to use the deck. Directions are available in myriad published books. Because the Universal Forces of Light want us to tap in to our spiritual guidance as quickly as possible, many intuitives and artists (including me) have been instructed to create modern and accessible versions of the ancient tarot system. Therefore, there are now many oracle decks available that are quite straightforward, including my *Ask Your Guides* deck, which is based on the minor arcana of a traditional tarot deck and is very easy to follow.

No matter what deck you choose to work with, you connect to your guides by asking questions and taking cards from the deck for answers. There are many ways in which an oracle deck can speak to you. The first is a one-card response to a question. You simply pose a question or focus on an issue and pull a single card for insight. For a more in-depth understanding of a question, you can pull several cards, laying them out in specified patterns.

I've had tremendous success with oracle decks and find that they serve as fantastic conduits. They're also especially useful for transmitting guidance on emotional issues in which you cannot be neutral or unbiased, such as whether or not to continue dating someone you've just met and like but don't necessarily trust, or whether or not to buy a house you love but cannot necessarily afford. They allow you to bypass the subjective part of your brain that wants to hear exactly what you want to hear and give you a more objective perspective. Having said this, I do think it unwise to consult an oracle or try to engage your guides when you're emotionally charged. It's far too easy to misinterpret their signals or, in the case of an oracle, ignore what you receive, if you're in a worked-up state of mind. If you're willing to be open to an objective higher influence, however, the cards will work well.

Again, it's a matter of what you intend. Are you looking for answers, or do you just want to hear what you want to hear? If you're seeking real guidance, the cards will work. If you're just looking for quick fixes or sympathy, they won't.

The beauty of tarot is that by using images instead of words, it speaks directly to our subconscious mind and links it directly to our higher consciousness. Tarot cards open a dialogue with the Universe and give you access to greater creativity. The great psychologist Carl Jung once said that if he were locked in prison and allowed only one thing, he'd choose the tarot, for in it lies the wisdom of the Universe.

If you'd like to explore using oracle decks, start by choosing one that appeals to your spirit. You can select one or several, as dialogue with the spirit is an art and not a perfect science. Because I love the cards so much, I have a whole collection and use them all at different times.

Certain decks seem to direct the conversation toward one specific subject; others deal with other subjects. For example, a classic tarot deck such as the Rider-Waite deck may address spiritual issues in depth, but be confusing when you ask for direction or guidance on whether or not to take a trip. An angel deck may offer you tremendous soul direction when dealing with difficult emotional issues, but leave you less satisfied when asking about a job.

I've created several divination decks myself because of this very distinction. My *Trust Your Vibes* deck is designed to help you make decisions and develop and strengthen your intuitive muscles, while my *Ask Your Guides* oracle deck is designed to directly strengthen dialogue with your guides. I also have a divination deck designed to help you with your soul purpose and soul lessons soon to be released, and I may create others.

A client named Betsy called me with great excitement to tell me that she used my *Trust Your Vibes* deck to help her write a children's book. Every time she got stuck or became insecure, she pulled a card from the deck, and before she knew it, she found herself encouraged enough to finish it. Then she began to use my *Ask Your Guides* deck to help get the book published. Before she contacted a potential publisher or agent, she pulled a card on whether or not that person or publisher would be the one to give her book the chance it deserved. To her utter surprise and delight, just by consulting the deck, she landed an agent on her third submission and sold the book within two months of completion. She assured me that without the cards guiding her, she would have most definitely lost courage and dropped the project before it was done. With their help, she was celebrating instead.

I have another client named Marcus who speaks directly to his guides every morning by shuffling and then pulling a single card from his classic tarot deck as he asks his guides to give him the psychic "weather report" for the day. One day he pulled the Tower card, a major arcana card designating upset and destruction. Later that day he was told by his boss that the company was being taken over by another, and his job was going to be eliminated by the end of the month. Ordinarily this would have sent him spiraling into terrible anxiety, but the early-morning warning prepared him just enough to handle it.

A subsequent pull of the cards yielded the Star, a card indicating that new surprises would emerge from the Universe. Marcus was later contacted by his brother-in-law, who asked him if he was interested in going into business with him running a fast-food Mexican restaurant in Iowa. As the Star card indicated, this came out of nowhere, and yet couldn't have come at a better time. The last I heard he was going for it, and still consulting with his guides day by day via the cards.

The key to using oracle decks for guidance is to play with several decks and see which one(s) work for you. Once you choose a deck, work with it for a while. Get familiar with it. Learn how to use it. Consider using a new deck like using a new computer, which allows you to communicate instantly with others around the world. Similarly, with an oracle-card deck, you can communicate across the Universe.

People have asked me if they must memorize the meanings of an oracle deck before they can consult it. Many divination experts would say yes, but I say no. I do think you should try to interpret your oracle directly before consulting your guidebook. What does your spirit see when looking at the card? What does your inner voice say? You can work with a guidebook, but trust your direct insights as well. And listen for your guides. You can even ask them how to interpret a card if you have no idea or can't fully understand its meaning. Reading a divination deck is an organic process, and you can experiment with various methods until you find one that suits you.

Never use your oracle deck insincerely. Don't laugh at an oracle or make fun of it in any way. If you do, you'll attract low-level entities, instead of higher-level spirit guides which, as I've mentioned before, are inclined to give you jumbled, disturbing messages that will only confuse and upset you. Such riffraff is generally harmless, but it's useless psychic interference and not to be invited in by careless consultations.

I'm not saying that you can't enjoy using divination decks. Indeed, you should, as they can be a great source of comfort and direction. Just be sincere, that's all.

I had a client named MK who used my deck to ask about her purpose in life. It suggested that she would have something to do with children and writing. It was nothing that even remotely interested her and made no sense at the time. Yet, a year later she was suddenly struck in the middle of the night with an idea to write an adult book in a children's format, and she became consumed with the project. Six months later, she'd written a beautiful book called *Will You Dance? . . . A Children's Story for Adults.* Now she's using it to teach self-esteem workshops for adults all over the country, just as the oracle had suggested.

You can consult a divination deck every day, if you like, but only once per question. Only if circumstances change can you consult the oracle again on the same subject. For example, I consulted my cards on whether or not to enroll my daughter in a certain school last year, when suddenly I was guided to homeschool her instead. Even though the cards said the school in question would be fine for my daughter, the new circumstances warranted a second look. The second consultation championed the idea of homeschooling and was much more enthusiastic than the first. Based on that feedback, she was homeschooled, and for the first time in her life she said that she loved learning.

I use my divination decks all the time because they're efficient and fun. But just because they're fun doesn't make their wisdom any less profound or my intention any less sincere. It's exciting and enjoyable to get instant feedback and saves wear and tear on your spirit. But how effective your divination is depends on you and not the deck. The more receptive you are, the more you can expect it to work for you as a means of communication between you and your guides.

Did You Know That . . .

. . . all divination decks are relevant, and it's strictly a matter of preference which one speaks to you.

Your Turn

Shuffle your cards thoroughly before using them. This infuses your deck with your personal vibration and attracts your guides. Get a feel for your cards, and see if you can sense their presence as you shuffle. Don't allow anyone else to use them. Keep them in a safe place, preferably wrapped in silk or satin to protect and preserve a clear vibration. Get comfortable with your deck, and treat it respectfully and as a friend. It's a tool that you will come to love if you work with it properly.

When you're ready to consult the deck, focus on your questions and concerns, one at a time, as you shuffle. With a single question in mind, select cards from the deck and then follow the guidebook in how to interpret the oracle cards. As with all guidance, be certain not to phase your question "Should I . . ." Instead, say, "Show me my options and all I need to know on this subject." Then engage the oracle for insight and direction.

Use your oracle deck as a springboard to directly connect with your guides, and be open to this guidance even if it doesn't make perfect sense the minute it comes through. Give the oracle a chance to play out. Usually the guidance becomes clear over time. Oracles make you aware of what your conscious mind doesn't know and should.

Now that you've learned how your guides work best with you, let's move on and focus on how to gracefully live a spirit-guided life.

PART VI

Living a
Spirit-Guided Life

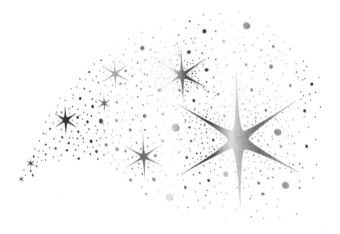

Chapter 28

Your Higher Self: The Greatest Guide of All

Of all the guides you have, the most important is your own Higher Self, the voice and frequency of your Divine, fully realized, eternal self, your direct link to your Creator, God. It's the most powerful, concrete, loving, immediate connection you have to all that you desire, all that you are here to learn and to contribute.

The primary task of your other guides and your angels is to help strengthen your conscious connection to your Higher Self so that it, rather than your limited, fear-based ego, runs your life. The other guides feel successful when your Higher Self sees through your eyes, interacts with others, makes your decisions, and evaluates your progress.

The voice of your Higher Self, as opposed to your other guides, is the most authentic you guiding you. When you're connected to your Higher Self, there are no other voices in your head. You're focused solely on how to be a more creative, joyful being. Your ego concerns fall by the wayside while your heart expands.

The way to view your other guides is to consider them as messengers and coaches who assist you in life's matters while leading you to your true self. Your Higher Self, on the other hand, is not a messenger, but the highest expression of you. Your guides are the middlemen; your Higher Self is the direct source of who you really are. Your guides' job is to connect you to your Higher Self; your Higher Self's job is to connect you to God.

When working with your guides, you must not turn yourself over and expect them to run your life. When connecting with your Higher Self, it's not only right to turn your power over, but desirable to do so, as it's not an outside source, but the real you.

A client asked me why we need all these other guides if his Higher Self is so powerful. The answer is that you don't. Their only role is assistance, support, companionship, and delight. They're optional, but not essential, helpers in your life's journey. On the other hand, you do need your Higher Self. Without it, you're lost, and consumed with fear and anxiety, as those who are disconnected with or unfamiliar with their higher selves will surely attest. Your ego takes over, and insecurity and doubt consume you. In spite of all of your ego's strategies to avoid this fate, it will never succeed in avoiding death. Even if you become rich, famous, and powerful, you cannot escape the inevitability of death. The more the ego tries, the worse you feel.

The ego thrives on control, so it isolates you from others through stories, projections, and judgments about others and yourself. It will use everything it can to keep you from feeling vulnerable or asking for guidance. In addition, the maneuvers of the ego are so exhausting and futile that they leave you with little energy left to experience and enjoy the wonders of life. You become weak, fatigued, sick, and old very quickly. There's no way around it—being run by your limited, fear-driven ego is guaranteed to ruin your life.

The only antidote for this terminal soul sickness is to connect to the voice and vibration of your Higher Self and let it lead. It is the self that doesn't die, but lives eternally and simply.

How do you connect with your Higher Self? The first step is to quiet the voice of your ego. You know the voice I mean, the one that rants, blames, defends, judges, justifies, whines, doesn't forgive, never forgets, expects the worst, and trusts no one. Until that voice is muted, you will not hear your Higher Self.

More than all other guidance, the voice of your Higher Self is very subtle, at least in the beginning, when you first connect. Once you do, the signal gets stronger and stronger and becomes hard to ignore. It's like tasting sugar for the first time; it's so sweet, so compelling, and so desirable that you want more.

The best way to hear your Higher Self and quiet your ego chatter is through meditation—taking 10 to 15 minutes a day to rest your brain, allay your fears, and consciously shift your focus. It's not difficult to do. All that's necessary is to stop relating to the outer world for that time and to turn inward to your breathing, inhaling slowly to the count of four, exhaling slowly to the count of four. That's it.

If your mind drifts, don't be upset. Just continue rhythmically breathing. It's a simple exercise, but it does take discipline and practice. The mind doesn't want to be controlled, so it will fight you. You must be prepared for that and resolve to stick to it every day, preferably at the same time. The more you practice on a schedule, the easier it becomes. Your subconscious mind will adjust to the routine and automatically carry out your intention. If you're consistent, in a couple of weeks you'll actually look forward to it.

Second, begin what I call meditative practices. By this I mean doing things with the intention of quieting your mind—going for a walk, folding the laundry, knitting, gardening, or painting—diverting your attention from mind chatter and giving you a break.

These two practices will always connect you to your Higher Self. They will help you to recognize and trust that you have a Higher Self that can successfully lead your life, to take full responsibility for it, and to stop giving your power away or blaming others for running your life.

When you connect to your Higher Self, you immediately know when you're off course. It may signal to you through your body, knocking on your heart, tapping on the back of your brain, and rumbling around in your belly until you pay attention. In these ways, your Higher Self keeps you from feeling good and at peace in your skin when you take a detour.

Like a pebble in your shoe or a sliver in your finger, your Higher Self conveys irritation and discomfort when you're being less than your authentic, loving, eternal self.

Unfortunately, so many people are willing to live with this discomfort that they ignore it or go to a great deal of trouble to cover it up by distracting themselves through external preoccupations, even addictions.

But the day you decide you're unwilling to ignore these signals, the day you decide to do whatever it takes to get on track, that's the day your connection to your Higher Self kicks into full gear. And when you surrender your ego over to your Higher Self, that's the day your life begins to work.

Another way to connect is to train your subconscious mind to bypass your ego and surrender control to your Higher Self by simply saying aloud, "Subconscious mind, take me now and always to my Higher Self." Whenever you feel anxious, upset, insecure, angry, hurt, confused, vengeful, or insignificant, repeat that phrase.

To strengthen the connection even more, every morning before opening your eyes say, "Subconscious mind, let my Higher Self, and only my Higher Self, lead me this day."

My friend Nelson used this strategy as he was ending an acrimonious marriage. Although both he and his wife agreed that it was time to go their separate ways, their egos continued to flare. The most challenging decision was to sell the house and split the money evenly. The day they put the house on the market, they were offered the full asking price in a cash deal with only two stipulations—that they accept the offer in two days and vacate within 30 days. Nelson was ecstatic, ready to move on with his life. He was sure his wife would be, too. Instead, she said no and didn't want to cooperate in any way.

He was furious; it was she who first wanted the divorce. Afraid to lose the deal, his ego wanted to go after her full force. He called me and asked what to do.

I told him to turn the issue over to his Higher Self. "But I have no time," he said. "We have to give the buyer an answer by tomorrow. Turning it over to my Higher Self is a fine philosophy, but my Higher Self can't make my ex-wife sign the deal."

"Turn it over to your Higher Self," I repeated. He remained quiet for a full five minutes.

"What does your Higher Self suggest?" I asked.

"It says do nothing," he said.

"Can you go along?" I said. "After all, it makes sense to me. You can't do anything. Your wife needs to come to terms with this on her own."

"I guess that's smart," he conceded. "I could never make her do a thing before, so why now?"

So he did nothing, as he was advised. Ten minutes before the deadline, she called. All she said was, "I accept the deal" and hung up. The next day the papers were signed and the house was sold without another angry word. His Higher Self was right.

My client Mary Ellen was beside herself with conflict when she accidentally discovered that her boss and two other workers were stealing funds from the investment company where she worked. She loved her job, but she was the newest employee, the only woman, and clearly not well liked by many of her male colleagues. She was afraid to say anything and possibly be attacked for it, but if she kept her mouth shut, she could be implicated as part of the crime.

She called me, upset, worried, indignant, and fearful about what to do.

"What does your Higher Self suggest?"

"I don't know. My Higher Self isn't talking. If I confront my boss, I'll lose my job; I'll be a whistle-blower and no one else will hire me."

Again I said, "Quiet your fears and tell me what your Higher Self suggests."

After a long silence, she said, "My Higher Self says resign in writing and tell my boss and his boss why, without naming names, and trust I will find another job."

A month passed and the thefts continued to bother her. Finally, she couldn't stand it, and she followed her Higher Self's advice and wrote the letter. She left without severance pay or a recommendation. She didn't dare ask for either.

Three months later, her old firm contacted her. They had fired her boss and the two employees and wanted to rehire her with a raise. No one ever mentioned her resignation or her accusations.

Trusting your Higher Self and bypassing your ego will initially feel like jumping off a cliff blindfolded. Your ego wants you to feel that way so it can stay in control. What you discover, however, if you decide you're willing to jump off that cliff, is that as spirit, you can fly. You become free of your ego's fear and begin to live as your spirit wants you to.

Did You Know That . . .

. . . choosing to follow the guidance of your Higher Self gives you more freedom than you ever imagined was possible? It allows you to live an authentic, loving, fearless life. Nothing gives you more power than that. Just decide you want your Higher Self to run your life, and say so in no uncertain terms. It's the most direct way to realize all your dreams.

Your Turn

The best way to get in touch with your Higher Self is to meditate. Meditation is a learned skill. Start by taking in a slow breath right now. Notice how your awareness expands by simply taking in more breath. Do it again. This time inhale to the count of four, hold it for a moment, and then exhale to the count of four. Don't rush. Take your time. Continue this until you establish a comfortable pace. If you'd like, you can listen to music, especially the baroque variety, which has the same number of beats per minute as deep meditation to help you relax your mind.

Continue to breathe like this until you achieve a slow rhythm. While breathing, simply repeat the phrases "I am" on the inhalation and "at peace" on the exhalation. If your mind begins to wander, don't worry about it. That's normal. Simply refocus on your breath and go back to the phrases "I am" (inhale) and "at peace" (exhale). That's it. You're meditating. Engage in this practice 15 minutes every day. In a week or so, you'll look forward to meditating because it quiets your mind. And when your mind is quiet, you begin to get in touch with your spirit.

Chapter 29

Following Your Guides Can Be Challenging

The greatest challenge you'll face when working with your guides is to accept and trust what they tell you, especially when nothing in the world seems to confirm what you're receiving. Living an intuitive, six-sensory, guided life takes courage. The guides will point out the best possible way to fulfill your path and purpose and make day-to-day life easier, but it's still up to you to decide whether to follow their input.

I had a client named Paul who was a wonderful medium and psychic working a day job in a bakery in New Jersey. He was happily married and a father of two, but extremely unhappy at work. His guides advised him to move to Columbus, Ohio, where his sister lived, and open a professional psychic practice.

The thought both thrilled and scared him to death at the same time.

What a dream come true! he thought. *What a wonderful way to serve others! But how will I pay my insurance? How will I ever buy a house?*

The outside world thought he was crazy and said don't do it, but his wife said, "Let's go for it." So, with no guarantees, he quit, telling his boss he was a psychic and that he had another path to follow. Not only did his boss accept his resignation gracefully, he became Paul's first client. A few short months into his new life, he was offered a chance to be on the radio. He was such a success that he was asked again and again. Soon after, people started contacting him for readings, and his career blossomed. By the end of the year, he was fully engaged as a psychic medium. Listening to his guides was challenging because it seemed like such a risk, but when he decided to work with them and trust their advice, it proved to be the best decision he could have ever made.

Another client, Jocelyn, a widow, had wonderful guides who spoke to her all the time. They advised her to take a cruise with her girlfriends during the Christmas holidays even though it would stretch her budget to the limit. Her sons thought she was frivolous and severely criticized her for going, saying she was being very irresponsible. She worried that they were right and set out to cancel her reservation, but her guides screamed "No!" At the last minute, she went ahead with her plans. To make sure her sons didn't rain on her parade, she even refused to let them take her to the airport.

On the cruise, she met a wonderful man who lived only three miles from her. He was a widower and a recently retired chiropractor, and the two of them hit it off immediately. Their relationship continued after the cruise. Two years later they married. The best part is that her sons grew to love him. He was a blessing all the way around. She occasionally teases her sons about advising her to stay home. They deny that they ever said that.

Did You Know That . . .

. . . working with your guides is a way of life? Choosing to accept and embrace help from higher sources means leaving behind the old life of fear and lack of control. Those who do leave, at least from my experience, have a far more blessed, synchronistic, abundant, joyful life.

Your Turn

It can be difficult, even scary, to follow your guides when everything and everyone around you tells you not to. All I can suggest is that you trust what you feel, listen to your heart, and don't ask others for their input. After all, spirit guidance is of the highest level, so there's no need to comparison shop. If you have doubts, outside opinions will only confuse you more. If you do trust your guidance, however, wonderful things will begin to unfold—perhaps not as quickly as you'd like, but they will unfold.

Chapter 30

Good News vs. Guidance

It's very important when working with your guides to be open to what you receive and not edit their messages to fit your agenda. Needless to say, we seek spiritual guidance to help us attain positive outcomes and happy endings. But the way to get to those positive outcomes and happy endings may be very different from the way you want to get there. The whole point of seeking guidance is to open yourself to new ways of seeing things and to accept new information that can influence your understanding of a situation so that you can then make better decisions. What doesn't work is when you only want your guides or Higher Self to agree with you or support your established way of thinking, even if it's inaccurate.

One of the most challenging aspects of seeking guidance is receiving it even when what it's difficult to hear and accept.

I had a client who consulted her guides about her marriage by way of an oracle deck and received dire warnings of loss, deceit, and betrayal.

Upset at the information, she threw the deck away. Her husband, an investment banker and trader, was according to her, "the epitome of dignity," and would never let her down. Besides, there was no chance of an affair. He was home every night, and she knew he was faithful. You can imagine her shock when several months later he was arrested for insider trading and misappropriation of funds and eventually sentenced to five years in prison.

Mortified and hurt beyond belief that he would bring such shame upon himself and his family, not to mention financial ruin, she said to me, "That stupid deck warned me. I should have never used it," as though the deck were to blame for her husband's fall from grace.

"That's an interesting perspective," I said. "It seems to me your guides tried to warn you through the deck. Why be angry at the warning? Your guides were advising you to take notice and possibly even discuss concerns such as betrayal and deceit with your husband. And you threw it away. Did you ever suspect any of this in advance?"

"Well, yes," she admitted sheepishly. "He had been acting unusually stressed, flying off the handle a lot, and seeming to shut down—not his normal self. That's why I consulted the deck in the first place. I felt something was off and wanted to find out more."

"Well, given your reaction, I'd say you made the classic mistake of shooting the messenger when you threw away the cards and ignored your guides," I said.

"What would you have done?" she asked defensively.

"If it were me, given the situation, I'd confront my husband and say I had bad vibes and ask what he was up to."

"I thought about it, but I was afraid. To tell the truth, I didn't want to know. We were living beyond our means, but I was too comfortable to ask questions. I only wish I had."

"Given that he's now off to jail, I bet your husband wished you had, too."

So, when asking for guidance, not only true for oracles, the cardinal rules are: Don't ask questions if you don't want to know the answers, and if the advice isn't to your liking, don't shoot the messenger.

Your guides can only give you the truth, at least high-level ones anyway. How you choose to use the information is up to you. If you receive negative information, be honest with yourself before you react. Are you doing anything, or is anyone around you, doing anything to invite such negativity? Are you in denial about anything, or using poor judgment or ignoring something that could come back to haunt you? Are you keeping company with anyone who disturbs or distresses your spirit? If so, pay attention. At least, that's what the guides are suggesting you do.

In my 37 years of doing readings, I can honestly say I've never truly surprised any client when sharing difficult or bad news from their guides. Our awareness is far keener than we admit, and we tend to blot out unpleasant realities. Guides can't and won't, however. So if you ask, the guides will answer, but it will be unbiased and not necessarily what you want to hear.

In another case, I had a client who said, "Whatever you do, don't give me any bad news. I can't take it."

Complying, I didn't tell her that her job was about to come to an end (which I saw), but instead encouraged her to follow her vibes and begin to look for her dream job as soon as possible because the time was right for getting it. Ten days later she was laid off and called me, screaming that I should have warned her.

"Given the restrictions you'd placed on me," I said, "I tried. We spoke of your work at length, and you were advised by your guides to seek a new job. Now you know why." She angrily hung up. Three weeks later I got a postcard saying she'd just landed a terrific new job and was sorry she'd overreacted.

It's very tempting to discard guidance that doesn't flatter you or complement your perspective, especially when using an oracle. I've had clients shuffle the deck and pull cards for guidance, only to throw what they get aside if it doesn't appeal to them. One woman, Gina, pulled three cards from her tarot deck while asking a question about opening her own restaurant. The guides warned her against moving too fast and forging unstable partnerships with the wrong people, advice she didn't want to hear. Having made up her mind about the business and partners before asking the oracle, she was visibly annoyed when the guides suggested she change her plans.

She stormed ahead anyway, signing a lease on the first site she found and forming a partnership with a man she hardly knew. The restaurant flopped after seven months, and she's now suing her partner for leaving her with the debt. She came back to see me, demoralized at her failure, not believing what had happened.

"You were warned," I reminded her. "You just didn't want to hear it."

"I know," she lamented. "I wasn't willing to listen. I just wanted you to tell me I was brilliant and would succeed."

That's why my teacher Charlie always told me never to ask for guidance unless I was truly open to receiving answers. If you ask for guidance but constantly ignore it, your guides see you as insincere and step away, as in the story of *The Boy Who Cried Wolf.*

Did You Know That . . .

. . . not being receptive to guidance is perhaps the greatest obstacle you'll have to overcome if you want to communicate with your guides? After all, it's hard to receive suggestions if your mind is made up.

Your Turn

The best way to ensure good rapport with your guides and establish ease and flow in communicating with them is to practice this four-step process:

- **Step 1:** Be open to guidance. This means begin each day with a receptive heart and mind for receiving guidance.

- **Step 2:** Expect guidance. Like everything else you expect in life, the more you expect it, the more you attract it.

- **Step 3:** Trust the guidance you receive. Speak your guidance out loud every chance you get, and listen to how it feels as you do. (It isn't quite the same if you write it down, but this is another way to create ease and flow with guidance.) Even if you're warned, or receive difficult news, once you express it out loud you'll be able to feel if it's accurate and feel relieved when it's acknowledged. If the guidance is sound, you'll feel it the minute you voice it, so do.

- **Step 4:** Start acting on your guidance as soon as you receive it. It may feel as though I'm inviting you to jump off a cliff, but I'm not. It's far more frightening, I think, to ignore your guides and move in the wrong direction than to act on your guidance. This takes practice, so ease into it. Take your time and have fun with it. Start by acting in small ways until you get comfortable trusting your guides and see positive results. Then move on to serious questions. Soon you'll be in constant rapport with your guides and in constant ease and flow in your life. Trust me, it works.

Chapter 31

Finding Believing Eyes

When learning to trust your guides, it can be very helpful to engage a receptive friend or two with whom you can comfortably share your guidance. You're looking for support here, not for someone to judge or question the guidance you receive. They should be open-minded, "believing-eyes" people—those who understand and encourage you to listen to your guidance, while at the same time know you well enough to identify whatever issues you have that may interfere with clear reception.

I was very fortunate when growing up to have a mother and many siblings with whom I could freely speak about my guides without fear of being censored or laughed at. When I was feeling stressed, insecure, or unclear concerning my guides' input or my ego's fears, my mom or one of my siblings would help clear up my confusion by simply listening as I talked it out.

I was also helped by my teacher Charlie, who didn't verify my guidance as much as he encouraged me to trust what I received, however subtle and vague, and to accept everything that came through my many developing intuitive channels.

I also had, and still have, girlfriends, such as my mentors Lu Ann and Joan, my closest friend Julia Cameron, and my shaman friend Debra Grace. And of course I have my husband, Patrick; and my daughters, Sonia and Sabrina. The four of us talk about our guides as comfortably as we talk about the weather. Being able to share my relationship with my guides is a major factor in strengthening that relationship and connecting to them every day.

Perhaps you already have people with whom you can openly talk about your experiences with your guides. If so, you know how important it is.

But if you're just entering the exciting and wonderful world of guides and don't have anyone to share with, ask your spirit helpers to bring you someone to fill the bill. One of the quickest ways to identify who's right for you and who isn't is to get some oracle cards, such as my *Ask Your Guides* deck, openly display it, and let your family and friends know that this is your new interest. Those who can offer encouragement and support will do so right away. Those who scoff won't share your interest, so don't try to change their minds, because you won't. Rather, spend your energy seeking out people who don't need convincing.

Connecting with guides is a very subjective experience; rarely do opposing views meet in the middle. Use common sense and careful observation before discussing your experience with others. Don't sabotage the delicate, energetic connection you're forging with your guides by allowing someone to bombard you with negative perceptions.

Did You Know That . . .

. . . you can engage support by openly talking about your guides, sharing what you feel or receive from them. The key to your success here lies in how you discuss your experience. If you're matter-of-fact, positive, and appreciative, much like talking about a new friend, you'll recruit interest and belief from the right people. Don't waste time arguing with those who show no interest.

Your Turn

I believe that having people with whom you can share your involvement with your guides is so fundamental to your success that I've initiated chat groups through my online courses in which people all over the world can share guide experiences. They've proven to be of tremendous value in helping people live a more comfortable, six-sensory life.

I also have a weekly radio show that invites people to share their guide connections through **www.hayhouseradio. com**™, or my Website: **www.trustyourvibes.com**.

There's a section of my Website where people can post their psychic stories for all to read and draw support from. I invite you to participate in all these connections.

These are just a few ways to introduce you to "believing eyes" of your own and help you pull back the energetic veil between the third and fourth dimensions. This will help make communication with your guides easy and natural. Openly seeking support may seem like a risk, but it will be far outweighed by the rewards you receive from like-minded believers.

Afterword

Thank Your Guides

When working with your guides, it's crucial that you openly show your appreciation for their assistance and thank them for all they do.

This pleases them very much, because it acknowledges that they're been successful in their efforts to support you and ease your way. Even more important to them is that by taking the time to appreciate and acknowledge their help, you expand your heart and the capacity to receive their love and Divine support. And the more you do so, the more they work to guide you, and the more you can be guided.

There are many ways to thank your guides. The easiest, of course (and easiest to forget), is to just say, "Thank you, guides," out loud every time you experience their help. Or, better yet, you can thank them in advance. A simple thank-you goes a long way in the realm of spirit, for it acknowledges your guides' presence in, and contribution to, your life and affirms the Divine Plan that wants to support your soul's growth in every way.

I've found, however, that the guides are especially delighted and receptive when the thank-yous take on a little more ceremony.

For example, every time my guides deliver a particularly blessed event or assist me in a significant way, even if only to distract me from too much worry or inspire me with a new idea, I like to show appreciation by lighting a favorite stick of incense in their honor. When I do, I tell them, "This incense is for you because I so appreciate all you do for me."

Another way I reward my guides is to offer them fresh flowers, an idea that came to me during my first visit to India 20 years ago. Whenever we visited a temple, women were outside selling marigolds to present to the gods. These gorgeous garlands were gifts to honor them, and because they were intended solely for Divine pleasure, the offering wasn't acceptable if the giver smelled the flowers. This floral gift wasn't new to me. I grew up as a Catholic, and every May 1 we offered beautiful flowers to Mother Mary in honor of, and gratitude for, her love and support.

Taking this theme into my heart, I offer bouquets to my guides, especially those who help me with my readings, by placing fresh flowers in my office every day. In keeping with the notion that they're for my guides' pleasure and not mine, I refrain from sniffing them directly, although I do enjoy the scent that fills the room.

I also thank my guides by lighting scented candles, another loving tradition I carried over from my Catholic upbringing.

Every week, when I went to church, I saved a part of my allowance so I could put a quarter in the offering box and light a candle to St. Thérèse, who I felt was my special guide Rose. To this day, I light both 7- and 14-day votive candles in appreciation of my guides.

Another wonderful way to express gratitude for your guides' help is to sing them a beautiful song or play them a lovely piece of music. Songs and instrumental music create a high-level harmony vibration that guides love to enter.

Yet another way to acknowledge your guides is to create an altar for them, and on it place images, photos, and icons of all that you love. I built my first altar at the foot of my bed when I was 12 years old. It held my first-communion rosary, a picture of my family taken at Christmas, a copy of my straight-A report card from the third grade, a drawing of my guide Rose, some dried lilac petals from the bush in our front yard, a small white votive candle in a glass container, and a bell. I rang the bell whenever I wanted my guides to come.

I still maintain an altar in my office; it takes up nearly an entire wall. It holds sacred things I've acquired from all over the world during the past 35 years. It's no longer just an altar; it's a shrine filled with holy and happy images, pieces of art, and various objects that remind me of my blessings. Standing in front of it not only draws in my guides, but also reinforces my close personal connection to Christ, Mary, and God.

To create an altar of your own, select a table or stand and place it in some area of a frequently visited room that won't be disturbed. Designate this as your spirit altar, and cover it with symbols, photos, and things that invoke a sense of happiness, peace, and love. Experiment with various objects, and see which ones raise your vibration, open your heart, and summon in you a deep sense of appreciation. Try sacred and personal photos, bells, flowers, candles—even a small mirror because it reflects light and you.

Another way to show appreciation is to keep a clean and organized home. If that's asking too much, at least maintain the area around your altar in this manner. This shows your respect for the guides by giving them a peaceful, clear place to rest. It also gives you surroundings conductive to communicating with them. An altar establishes a meeting point with your guides, and the calmer and cleaner it is, the clearer the channel through which you will connect.

If you find that your guides have been particularly supportive, reward them by creating a banquet in their honor. To do this, collect candles, fresh flowers, incense, happy photos, bells, and holy pictures, together with a written prayer of gratitude, and put it prominently on your altar. Let your guides know that this is a banquet for them to step forward and enjoy. It creates an incredibly high and powerfully charged vibration in your home, a gift that keeps on giving. You'll feel the Divine energies powering in to receive your gifts, leaving love and blessings.

Did You Know That . . .

. . . my teacher Dr. Tully once told me that the best thing you can do for others, for yourself, and for the world is to be happy? This is the best way to appreciate your blessings and your guides' support.

Your Turn

One of the highest ways to honor and appreciate your guides and all Divine helpers is to focus on living with a happy heart and a positive outlook and leaving your fears in their care. In this way, not only do you accept your Divine blessings, but you also become a guide and blessing to others.

May God bless you, and your angels protect you.
May your runners connect you, your helpers assist you,
your healers support you, your teachers enlighten you, your joy
guides delight you, the nature spirits balance you, your animals
guides
recall your soul, and your Higher Self lead you to live a life
of peace, grace, creativity, and contribution filled with
love and laughter on your personal earthly journey.

With all my love and support,
Sonia

Acknowledgments

I'd like to thank my mother, Sonia Choquette, for parting the veil to the world of spirit and introducing me to the love of the heavens. And to my father for being the steady ground in my highly spirited world. To my husband, Patrick; and daughters, Sonia and Sabrina, for your perpetual love, patience, and willingness to understand my life's work. To Lu Ann Glatzmaier and Joan Smith for being my "believing eyes" and soul sisters for as long as I can remember. To my teachers Dr. Tully and Charlie Goodman for sharing their wisdom and techniques with me for establishing the highest level of spirit-guided communication.

To Reid Tracy, my new Earth angel, and the entire staff at Hay House for your dedication and tireless support. To my creative "catcher's mitt" and beloved friend Julia Cameron for helping me bring this work into the world. To my editors Bruce Clorfene and Linda Kahn for helping me shape this book into a presentable manuscript, and to all my clients for lending me your stories. Above all, I'd like to thank God and all blessed beings of the Universe for your love, guidance, and hard work on my behalf as you perpetually guide me on my path. I am your grateful and humble servant.

About the Author

Sonia Choquette is a world-renowned author, storyteller, vibrational healer, and six-sensory spiritual teacher in international demand for her guidance, wisdom, and capacity to heal the soul. She's the author of eight best-selling books, including *Diary of a Psychic* and *Trust Your Vibes,* and numerous audio programs and card decks. Sonia was educated at the University of Denver, the Sorbonne in Paris, and holds a Ph.D. in metaphysics from the American Institute of Holistic Theology. She resides with her family in Chicago. Website: **www.soniachoquette.com**

Notes

Notes

Notes

Notes

Notes

Notes

Notes

Notes

Hay House Titles of Related Interest

Books

Ask and It Is Given, by Esther and Jerry Hicks
(The Teachings of Abraham)

Contacting Your Spirit Guide (a book-with-CD),
by Sylvia Browne

***David Wells' Complete Guide to Developing Your Psychic
Skills,*** by David Wells

Goddesses & Angels, by Doreen Virtue, Ph.D.

101 Ways to Jump-Start Your Intuition, by John Holland

The Unbelievable Truth by Gordon Smith

Card Decks

The Power of Intention Cards, by Dr. Wayne W. Dyer

Wisdom Cards, by Louise L. Hay

All of the above are available at your local
bookstore, or may be ordered by visiting:

Hay House UK: **www.hayhouse.co.uk**
Hay House USA: **www.hayhouse.com**®
Hay House Australia: **www.hayhouse.com.au**
Hay House South Africa: **orders@psdprom.co.za**
Hay House India: **www.hayhouse.co.in**

We hope you enjoyed this Hay House book.
If you would like to receive a free catalogue featuring additional
Hay House books and products, or if you would like information
about the Hay Foundation, please contact:

Hay House UK Ltd
292B Kensal Rd • London W10 5BE
Tel: (44) 20 8962 1230; Fax: (44) 20 8962 1239
www.hayhouse.co.uk

✻✻✻

Published and distributed in the United States of America by:
Hay House, Inc. • PO Box 5100 • Carlsbad, CA 92018-5100
Tel.: (1) 760 431 7695 or (1) 800 654 5126;
Fax: (1) 760 431 6948 or (1) 800 650 5115
www.hayhouse.com

Published and distributed in Australia by:
Hay House Australia Ltd • 18/36 Ralph St • Alexandria NSW 2015
Tel.: (61) 2 9669 4299; Fax: (61) 2 9669 4144
www.hayhouse.com.au

Published and distributed in the Republic of South Africa by:
Hay House SA (Pty) Ltd • PO Box 990 • Witkoppen 2068
Tel./Fax: (27) 11 467 8904 • www.hayhouse.co.za

Published and distributed in India by:
Hay House Publishers India • Muskaan Complex • Plot No.3
B-2 • Vasant Kunj • New Delhi – 110 070.
Tel.: (91) 11 41761620; Fax: (91) 11 41761630.
www.hayhouse.co.in

Distributed in Canada by:
Raincoast • 9050 Shaughnessy St • Vancouver, BC V6P 6E5
Tel.: (1) 604 323 7100; Fax: (1) 604 323 2600

✻✻✻

Sign up via the Hay House UK website to receive the Hay House
online newsletter and stay informed about what's going on with
your favourite authors. You'll receive bimonthly announcements
about discounts and offers, special events, product highlights,
free excerpts, giveaways, and more!
www.hayhouse.co.uk